William Callender

**Thrilling Adventures of William Callender, a Union Spy from Des Moines**

William Callender

**Thrilling Adventures of William Callender, a Union Spy from Des Moines**

ISBN/EAN: 9783337180188

Printed in Europe, USA, Canada, Australia, Japan

Cover: Foto ©ninafisch / pixelio.de

More available books at **www.hansebooks.com**

# THRILLING ADVENTURES

OF

## WILLIAM CALLENDER,

# UNION SPY

FROM DES MOINES.

DES MOINES:
MILLS & COMPANY, PRINTERS.
1881.

# NOTE BY THE EDITOR.

THE following pages embrace, in the form of an autobiography, a recital of the thrilling adventures of WILLIAM CALLENDER, a member of company D, Second Iowa Infantry, who was a scout for some time under General Dodge at Corinth and Pulaski, and afterward under General Stockweather. I have known the author many years, and am confident that he does not diverge, in a single instance, from the literal truth as he understands it from his point of observation. He tells his story in an artless and unaffected style, which must impress all readers with his earnestness, and his dominant love of truth. There is none of that personal vanity, which is too often found in works of this class. I venture to say that no other work, descriptive of personal adventure, which has been published in Iowa, will be found as attractive and absorbingly interesting as this.

For several reasons the Second Iowa Infantry achieved as high a historic reputation as any other regiment organized in Iowa. It was the first one sent from the State under the call which authorized its enlistment; and being first in the field, its march to the front was followed with profound anxiety by the hearts of its friends at home; and its deeds of valor, and its martyrs, were written up for publication by graphic reporters and given to the world at so early a date as to make this band of brave men illustrious before the numerous regiments organized in 1862 had any existence. The names of Generals Curtis, Crocker, Tuttle and Weaver, along with Colonels Mills and Baker, and Adjutant Godfrey, are, with many others, identified with this regimental organization; and of company D, the names of Ensign, Davis, Tunis, Dykeman, Marsh, and others, have gone into history in connection with the world's victorious heroes. Of these, several have already gone to their reward. Curtis died years ago; and in 1865, Crocker died at Washington; Mills and Baker fell at Corinth mortally wounded; and Dykeman died at Philadelphia two or three years since. The others, so far as I know, are living, as participants in the political blessings and franchises which their own arms and courageous spirits helped to create. The war has now receded from us nearly two decades, in point of time; and the period will soon come when the soldiers for the Union who survived the war will pass out of existence; and now, while many of them are still living, the opportunity is presented to take down their report from their own lips of the thrilling adventures through which they passed, when their lives were exposed to a storm of rebel bullets.

J. M. DIXON.

DES MOINES, June 15, 1881.

# CONTENTS.

## CHAPTER I.
### A PROPHETIC DREAM.

My Sister—Early Life—Removal to Des Moines—Trip to Denver—Going to War—Company D—Donelson and Shiloh—Strategy—Appointed a Scout. 9—16.

## CHAPTER II.
### FIRST SCOUTING ADVENTURE.

Harrison—Start Scouting—Railway Station—Dangerous Answer—My Fears—Rebel Horseman—Roddy's Command at Bay Springs—Our Success—The Deer Scare, and Return to Corinth—Harrison's Promotion. 17—21.

## CHAPTER III.
### HARRISON'S COMMAND.

Col. Newsome—George Noris—Citizen Moon—Three Rebels—Horses Shot—The Doctor—The Ambuscade—Fall from Horse—Mulharen's Mule. 22—25.

## CHAPTER IV.
### ADVENTURES AROUND FLORENCE.

Stop with Citizen—My Fellow Scouts—Capture of Seven Rangers—Our Captured Steeds—Servants in the Field—Angry Planter—Blackberry Cordial—Thrilling Charge—My Horse Killed—Miraculous Escape—Night Ambuscade. 26—33.

## CHAPTER V.

### THREE EXPEDITIONS.

Hensal—We Go to Ripley—Stop in Suburbs—Skirmish at Hotel—Capture Three Rebels—Drive Two Rebel Companies—Capture Town—Visit Des Moines—Back to War—Capture Job, the Guerilla—Capt. Stinnett's Guerillas—Strategy by Moonlight—A Jolly Prisoner Captured—Seizure of Horses. 34—43.

## CHAPTER VI.

### FOUR EXPEDITIONS.

War-widows at Sugar Creek—The Out-building—The Dark Night—Rebel Horsemen—Capture of Five Rebel Officers by Strategy—Their Mortification—Captain Hamm—The Bridge at Night—The Surprise—The Leap for Life—Lost in the Swamp—Escape—Capture of a Spy—Rebel Retaliation—Price on Hensal's Head—Brown's Treachery—Keeping the Appointment—Brown Outwitted—Union Women—In the Hands of the Rebels—Death Stares me in the Face—Charge of Union Troops—My Deliverance. 44—60.

## CHAPTER VII.

### A THRILLING CHAPTER.

The Conscript Sergeant—Pursued by Guerrillas—Flight through the Woods—Lost in the Forest—The Baying of Blood-hounds—The Raft—Swimming for Life—Startling Strategy on the Road—Reach Savannah—Form a Union Company—Sleeping in the Woods—Five Guerrillas Killed—Rebel Vengeance—We Lodge in Courthouse—Invaded by Guerrillas—The Warning Cry—An Awful Leap—Murder of my Friends—Fleeing to the Brush—My Blistered Feet—Kind Union Friends—Hulse and Britton—We Cross the River—In the Brush—Blood-hounds again—Leaky Skiff—More Friends—Horses Bought—Headed Off—Wander in Forest all Night—Kirk's Guerrillas—Return to Pulaski. 61—81.

## CHAPTER VIII.

### THE TWO EXPEDITIONS.

Trestle-work—In the Rebel Lines—Brown's Corral—Fun with Colored Men—The Comic Flight—The Block-house—Dispatch to Morgan—Rebel Cavalry Scared from Rogersville by Midnight Ruse—Dispatch to Rosseau—Two Recruits—Start for Pulaski—Pray for Darkness—House on Hill—Rebel Ambush—Bishop's Capture—The Retreat—The Path and the Hill—The Hot Pursuit—The Mantrap—Scaling the Hill—The Night-watch—Tracks in the Road—On to Pulaski—Bishop and his Mother. 81—88.

## CHAPTER IX.

### FOUR INCIDENTS.

James Holly—Rebels at Jumpertown—Pierce and his Company—Rebels in Line—The Signal Gun—The Traitor—Our Retreat—Scene at the Bridge—Capture of Pierce and his Men—Flag of Truce—The Guerrilla Chief—All Night with him—Lieutenant Gardiner—Parole of Pierce—Swim the River—The Man with the Portmanteau—Ten Thousand Dollars—Murphy—The Refugee—We Go to his Home—His Union Overcoat—Assault on his House by Guerrillas—Shot-gun and Revolver—The Fight from Door and Window—Defeat of Foes—Killed and Wounded—Expected Return of Guerrillas—Murphy's Sad Farewell and our Return to Corinth—An Old Rebel—Mischief against Him—Visit the Calvins—My Threat—Arrested as a Guerrilla—My Acquittal. 89—101.

## CHAPTER X.

### CLOSING ADVENTURES.

Run Down by Rebels—Leap from Horse—Old Colored Woman—Her Kindness—Sleep in Cotton-gin—Find Skiff—Escape—The Log and Bushes—Roddy's Army—The Rattlesnake—My Disgust—The Old Planter—The Three Daughters—The Little Strategy—The Brothers—A Miscarried Letter. 102—107.

## CHAPTER XI.

### THE HORRORS OF WAR.

Hood's Raid—Condemned Stock—Colored Exodus—Lost Children—Pontoon Bridges—Drowning of a Child—Reach Nashville—Hundreds Perish—Patience of the Colored Race. 108—110.

## CHAPTER XII.

### TRUE FIDELITY.

Minerva Perkins—Out of Money—At Athens—Down with the Typhoid Fever—No White Unionists—Three Friends—My Faithful Nurse—Her Sacrifices and Devotion—Recovery—Colored Troops at Huntsville—Send for Minerva—Chicken Pies—Restaurant Business Failure—Prospecting for Lead—Back to Des Moines—Send for Minerva again—Our Marriage. 111—114.

## CHAPTER XIII.

### REMARKS PERSONAL.

My Relation to the Army—Enlistment—Detailed as a Scout—Furloughed—Return to the Army—Offered a Lieutenancy—Statement of Captain Griffith. 115—116.

# THRILLING ADVENTURES.

## CHAPTER I.

### A PROPHETIC DREAM.

My Sister—Early Life—Removal to Des Moines—Trip to Denver—Going to War—Company D—Donelson and Shiloh—Strategy—Appointed a Scout.

EARLY in the war, while at St. Louis with my regiment, I had a singular dream, which I propose to relate. I thought that my sister Elizabeth, who died in Ohio thirteen years before, appeared to me, and while she looked at me affectionately, said:

"My brother, there are many trials and dangers before you; but if you do your whole duty you will escape unharmed, and come home safely at the end of the war."

Saying this, she passed from my sight; and then, by one of those sudden transitions which often occur in dreams, I imagined myself in the South, wandering blindly around among a group of old buildings, with the blackness of darkness enveloping the scene; I could not see my way out, and despair seemed to settle on my mind. Another change came, and darkness was succeeded by the blessed light of day. I was ascending the Mississippi River on a steamer, the water of which was as clear and transparent as crystal. Every object I saw was bathed in luminous and glorious light. The dream then ended, and when I awoke it was so photographed on my memory I knew it never would be forgotten. From that night the confidence I felt in my own safety could not be shaken during the war, and from that night, too, I was more than ever guarded in reference to my conduct and duty. As a soldier I tried to perform the most effective service, and never, at any time, was I under arrest, or even censured for disobedience of orders, or inefficiency, or anything else. My relation to other Union soldiers was always fraternal and kind. The dream I had at St. Louis was prophetic, and the reader already knows its interpretation. When at home on furlough I told the dream to my mother, whose faith in it saved her from many an hour of anxiety concerning her soldier son.

I was born in Defiance county, Ohio, in the year 1838. My parents were in very moderate circumstances and my early life in the Buckeye State was obscure and uneventful, marked by no incident of sufficient importance to merit a place in this narrative. Sometime before our removal to the West, and when I was about sixteen or seventeen years of age, I became acquainted with the daughter of a neighbor, named Sarah Cleland. To this estimable girl I became devotedly attached, and though the intimacy formed between us did not terminate in marriage, her memory has been enshrined in my heart, never to yield up its consecrated place. If the theory of guardian angel be true, I am confident that in times of peril and anxiety she has sustained that relation to me. \* \* \*
Thousands of times has vivid memory brought her back

into my presence from the long ago, encouraging me in life's weary pilgrimage.

In the year 1856 my father's family removed to Des Moines, Iowa, where I was engaged in active toil until the spring of 1860, when I went to Nebraska City. There I hired out as a teamster in Russell's train, bound for Denver, and transporting supplies to the infant settlements of the gold region. To my charge were confided six yoke of cattle.

Not long after starting on this trip the index finger of my left hand was attacked by a felon which gave me untold agony for many days and nights. Despite the pain I was enduring I carried out my resolution to go to Denver with the team, though the trip was 700 miles, and distinguished for hardship and peril. I was paid $20 a month for my services as teamster, and on my return to Des Moines, which occurred the same year, I transferred my entire earnings to my father, to help him along in his struggles to obtain a living for the family.

The spring of 1861 was signalized by the inauguration of the war for the Union. Early in that year the Second Iowa infantry was organized and sent to the front—company D of that regiment, to which I had the honor of belonging, was as illustrious, perhaps, as any other band of brave men ever sent from the State. The lamented Crocker belonged to it, as also did Noe W. Mills, and many other brave officers and men whose bodies are now slumbering in the graves of patriots.

Our regiment was sworn into service at Keokuk; not long afterward it was *en route* for Hannibal to do service in northern Missouri. The train on which our soldiers had embarked stopped for a brief time, one morning, at a small station between Hannibal and St. Joe. There a violent secessionist made his appearance, with pistol in hand, breathing threatenings and slaughter against the Yankee invaders. He was acquainted with a soldier in company A of our regiment, whose presence was the pretext for his volleys of insane abuse. In the midst of his crazy exclamations he was shot down, and his body, writhing in the agonies of death, was dragged by his mother backward into the house before which he had been standing just as the train was leaving the depot.

We tarried for a time at St. Joe, stemming the tide of hostility in that disaffected city. Finally we proceeded to Bird's Point, near Cairo, from which place, after the regiment had been somewhat depleted by hard service, we were ordered to St. Louis to recruit our decimated ranks. Some time before this latter movement was effected my acknowledged expertness in the care and control of animals took me from the ranks to assume the duties of teamster. In due time I reported to my regiment at St. Louis, from which place, after we had passed through the historic humiliation imposed on us for the alleged offenses of some of our boys in McDowell's College, we proceeded to Kentucky and Tennessee to participate in the grand victories which were subsequently achieved by the Union army under command of the man of destiny.

It was a chilly time in February when the regiment left the Cumberland River to find its way to Ft. Donelson, five miles distant. Not a blanket nor an ounce of provision did we take with us in this perilous expedition in an enemy's country. Unprotected as we were against the elements, it is not to be wondered at that the soldiers suffered intensely from the cold. The want of food, too, made our condition greatly worse. On the afternoon of the second day after our disembarkation two barrels of crackers were opened for the benefit of our famishing boys; and we were about to fall to to build up our wasted tissues when an order peremptorily came for the Second Iowa to charge the enemy. Colonel Tuttle was in command, and was, by the way, one of the bravest and best officers in the Union ranks. The charge made that day through the field, and up that hill at Donelson, and over fallen trees, and a thousand other obstructions which hostile ingenuity had placed in our way, and in the face, too, of a storm of leaden hail poured out upon us, perdition hot, from the beleaguered fortress, belongs not so much to this personal narrative as it does to the province of general history. One thing is certain, however, that but few of the crackers were eaten. Two hundred and fifty members of our regiment were included among the killed and wounded as a result of this fearful charge. It is certain also that three gallant Southern regiments, including the famous Mississippi Tigers, were literally swept out of existence on that day by the impetuous onslaught of the Second Iowa. It is true, too, that our regiment was the first to plant the standard of the Union over the hostile defenses of Fort Donelson. After the battle was over and the victory won rebel prisoners who had belonged to the three demolished regiments expressed a great desire to see that gallant band of men who had so effectually driven them from the field.

It was worthy of remark here that Col. Tuttle was made brigadier-general for his gallant services at Donelson. Theodore Weeks, a soldier from Des Moines, and one of the first to fall in defense of the Union flag, was shot through the temple and fell dead near my side.

His body and that of Sergeant Doty, both of company D, and both killed in this charge, were brought to Des Moines for interment, and both are slumbering in Woodland Cemetery.

On the night following this decisive charge I was placed on picket duty near the breastworks of the enemy. A mournful scene surrounded me in the dim obscurity. Rebels and Union men, some of whom were dead, and others dying, were here and there lying in their helplessness. A little distance from my post of duty Lieutenant Edgar Ensign, of company D, lay prone on the ground and suffering from a terrible wound. It was a cold night in February, and this circumstance made the experiences of that night all the more bitter and painful. Some time in the night, while pursuing my monotonous rounds, I came upon the body of a dead rebel whose canteen and haversack gave me a timely supply of water and provisions. I also appropriated his blanket, as he had no further use for it. It will be remembered that I had not eaten anything for many hours; and while a fellow-soldier and myself were engaged in stowing away these provisions we felt indeed grateful that the chances of war had so signally favored us.

Early the following morning Fort Donelson surrendered to the victors, giving to the loyal North the first grand triumph of the war, and proving to the rebel confederacy that if they succeeded in their mad attempt to break up the American Union they must do it by conquering soldiers as prompt to fight and as efficient with their weapons as themselves.

The army was transferred to the vicinity of Pittsburg Landing on the Tennessee River. Just before the battle of Shiloh took place some of the regiments—and among them I remember the Seventeenth Iowa—made the hills resound by many a song, gotten up for their amusement. In a spirited manner they sang the well-known hymn beginning with—

"On Jordan's stormy banks I stand," etc.

I told some of these patrotic ministrels that their tune would change before long. There was a general expectation that a great battle was imminent; and that expectation was soon realized. On the evening of that day thousands of Federal troops, driven to the margin of the Tennessee River, were ready, to all human appearances, to throw themselves into the water to escape the victorious charges of the enemy. Songs and hymns of triumph were converted into wails of agony. On that eventful evening, however, the vanguard of General Buell's reinforcing army, forty thousand strong, crossed the river to participate in the battle and in the grand victory for the Union on the morrow.

After this battle I was appointed wagon-master. For several months the regiment was stationed at Camp Montgomery, two and one-half miles from Corinth. One day while engaged in the duties pertaining to my office, several of my teamsters were attacked by a large body of Confederates. Being apprised of this sudden movement of the enemy I spurred back to the outskirts of our camp, where, as luck would have it, I found a number of stragglers and convalescents, whom, to the number of forty or fifty, I rallied in quick time and led them on to repel the charge. This counter-stroke of strategy was eminently successful. The rebels, numbering about 800, were pursuing our men through the woods; and as the trees intercepted their view it was easy for them to imagine our force to be greatly more formidable in numbers than the facts of the case really warranted. This circumstance threw them into a panic, and they fled in the wildest confusion, having done but little damage to our men or our property. A rebel major, who was an actor in this raid, reported afterward to his colonel that the soldiers under his command had fought against three Yankee regiments.

Not long after this spirited action a fellow soldier named Frank Harrison came to me with a request from General Grenville M. Dodge that I should accompany him (Harrison) on a scouting expedition to discover the whereabouts of the rebel General Roddy, who had established his headquarters in Tuscumbia valley, fifty or sixty miles from Corinth.

Here I will close the first chapter of my history, designing in the next to detail some of my thrilling experiences as a Union scout and spy.

# CHAPTER II.

### FIRST SCOUTING ADVENTURE.

Harrison—Start Scouting—Railway Station—Dangerous Answer—My Fears—Rebel Horseman—Roddy's Command at Bay Springs—Our Success—The Deer Scare, and Return to Corinth—Harrison's Promotion.

As the reader is aware, I was now entering on the performance of duties of the most thrilling and dangerous character, yet, nevertheless, there was a fascination about them which strongly invited rather than repelled adventure. In all military enterprises there is constant danger, but the army scout, occupying as he does a position outside of the general military system, literally takes his life in his own hands. If he be captured by the enemy he may expect no quarter. From time immemorial the laws of war have consigned the captured spy and scout to a prompt and ignominious death.

My first duty as a Federal scout was to discover, in company with Frank Harrison, hitherto mentioned, the whereabouts of the cruel and formidable rebel band under the lead of General Roddy. He had been raiding a large portion of the Tuscumbia valley, committing just such depredations as a guerrilla chieftain, during the war for the Union, would be expected to perpetrate. We started afoot on our perilous journey, moving through the woods as far as practicable, thus avoiding the highways, so that we might the more easily escape detection if we were cross-questioned by interviewing rebels. Our appearance was of the most simple kind, calculated in itself to deceive the most wary and vigilant of the enemy. It was understood beforehand, in case we were confronted and questioned by the enemy, that Harrison should pass himself off as quartermaster and I as wagon-master of the Second Iowa infantry. We would also represent ourselves as deserters, hastening southward to find protection within the Confederate lines. We footed it along for hours, mostly in the shadow of the luxuriant forests, meeting with no incident of any special moment.

Shortly after night-fall we came to an old railway station, twenty miles south of Corinth. The building was occupied by a man and his family, all of whom, I supposed, sympathized with the rebel cause. The man did not seem to be very curious or inquisitive. On our entrance into the house he accosted us with but one leading question, but this was fraught with significance to ourselves:

"Whar be you'ns from?"

"From Corinth," was the prompt, and I thought at the time fatal, reply of my companion. In my judgment he had inadvertantly given us both away to the enemy. His response was a wide departure it seemed from the programme on which we had started out, and though he was a loyal man and true, meaning all for the best, his answer to the question of our host for the night filled me with vague uneasiness and alarm.

As we were permitted to remain all night, we were conducted to bed upstairs, while the family remained below. About midnight, as nearly as I could guess, several rebel horsemen were heard somewhat noisily approaching the house. To say that I was not thrown into considerable trepidation by the circumstance would be a falsity with which I would not wish to soil this veritable history. Our host had the opportunity, as well as the ability, if he so desired, to hand us over to the tender mercies of those midnight marauders. Would he do it? We shall see. We lay profoundly quiet, with suppressed breathing and anxious hearts, while the riders dashed up to the house, called out our host, and held with him a somewhat prolonged interview. I expected every moment that a signal for our betrayal would be given, and was preparing to defend myself as best I could under the circumstances. Not long afterward we were gratified to hear the riders leave the premises, and as the man of the house was heard to shut the door and retire to bed, we thankfully returned to our slumbers, assured that the danger of the hour was past and gone. Next morning at day-break we left the house of our friendly host and proceeded on our way. As heretofore stated, it was our purpose to keep outside of the regular course of travel, thus avoiding any chance encounter with the enemy. At one time during the day we were moving along a little by-path when we were startled by the sudden approach of three Confederate horsemen. As we did not feel in a condition to invite questions or provoke hostilities, we decided that the best thing to do in this emergency was to escape recognition, if possible. The riders, it seemed, were coming down straight upon us, and in another moment we would be revealed to them without remedy unless we took immediate steps to avert this disaster. Fortunately for us a brier patch, many of which are found in the Sunny South, was close at hand; and into this we moved with great caution and celerity. Down we crouched among the encircling brambles, enduring the punctures of the sharp thorns as best as we could, while the rebel riders, wholly unconscious of our presence, passed within thirty feet of our hiding-place. When the danger was past we emerged from our retreat and went on our way.

About noon of this day we struck the main road and saw, some distance in advance, two horsemen. We followed on, and finally observed that one of the riders dismounted at a house, into which he was seen to go, while his companion moved on without halting. We proceeded at once to the house, and having obtained admission we saw in the room to which we were introduced, a man seated at a table engaged in refreshing himself with wholesome viands, while in a corner near by were his gun and blanket.

Without any preliminary remarks we asked the man at the table if he could direct us to the nearest Southern army. He appeared to be a rather unsuspicious person, and answered immediately that General Roddy had marched to Bay Springs on the Sunday preceding, and had left on the following day for Tuscumbia. In this interview we learned also that the locality called Bay Springs was only about two miles distant. Thus the object for which we were sent out from Corinth had been attained. We had found out what we desired to know in reference to Roddy's command, and all we had to do was to find our way back to Corinth as quickly as possible. To make a successful start for this destination we bade our friendly Southron farewell and set out as though we were heading for the

Springs. Arriving at a point which we deemed proper for our purpose we wheeled round and made northward for the Union lines.

At one place, I remember, as we were returning, a couple of deer started up before us with a crash and fled away into the forest. The suddenness of this movement threw me, for a moment, off my guard. I verily believed, on the instant, that we had been ambuscaded by a band of rebels, and the hair bristled on my head. After a little, however, we moved on, laughing at the harmless incident which had taken place. In due time we reached Corinth and reported to Gen. Dodge. Not long after these events Frank Harrison, my companion in these adventures, was made chief of scouts.

# CHAPTER III.

### HARRISON'S COMMAND.

Col. Newsome—George Noris—Citizen Moon—Three Rebels—Horses Shot--The Doctor—The Ambuscade—Fall from Horse—Mulharen's Mule.

SOME curiosity may be entertained by the reader to know something in reference to my personal appearance and qualities in those days of pluck, trial, and physical endurance. The fact has already been stated that I was young, and to a great extent, inexperienced. In person, I was neither tall nor heavy, but my form was erect and straight as an arrow. I was light, lithe and sinewy; and my activity, as will be demonstrated in future chapters, was somewhat remarkable; and the powers of endurance with which nature had invested me, were such as to give me every chance of success, when these elements were in demand. I may, therefore, say, without being charged with presumption, that I possessed those qualifications, in no mean degree, which are required in a scout and detective.

Within the next few days Gen. Dodge sent me on two excursions, both of which were executed successfully; but as neither of them was fruitful of any special or thrilling incident I will omit them both, being well aware that the enterprises yet to be narrated, will furnish material enough for a large volume. In my first trip I went afoot; but in nearly all subsequent ones I went horseback. I wore my hair long, according to the southern style; and my clothes also befitted that sunny clime. The broad pronunciation of the average Southron I adopted without difficulty; and in a very short time, by continued practice, I became in person, manner and speech a citizen or citizen soldier of the Southern Confederacy.

In the summer of 1863 Frank Harrison, whose name has appeared before in this volume, was engaged in raising a loyal regiment in West Tennessee. Having accomplished his work he was placed at the head of his new command, and was dispatched, with about four hundred men, to inflict punishment on the rebel Col. Newsome, who with his band of insurgents, was committing many depredations in portions of the State. In company with a fellow scout, named George Noris, I proceeded in advance of this expedition in search of such information as would be useful to the general cause. We traveled without interruption until we reach a point about seventy-five miles north of Corinth. The reader will understand that we wore the uniform of Confederate soldiers. At the point mentioned, we met a citizen of that section whose name was Moon. Of him we inquired, with all semblance of honesty, if he could tell us where our command was; referring, of course, to Colonel Newsome's regiment, which we knew would not be far away. The answer was, that the command we sought was encamped at a place about three-quarters of a mile distant.

We managed to keep the citizen in conversation until our own command under Harrison came up; and after the astonished Butternut, whom we were pumping, had been turned over as a captive Noris and myself dashed on ahead in pursuit of fresh glory. We rode about a quarter of a mile until we approached a place, with a field upon the left, and a forest on the right, and with a creek in front. A by-road emerged into the highway on our left between us and the stream. Just before reaching this intersection I distinctly heard the approach of horsemen who were moving toward the highway on the by-road, to which I have referred. We could not see them, but their loud talking and the resounding tread of their horses made their coming evident. I told Noris to remain where he was until the strangers revealed themselves at the corner of the fence, but George disobeyed instructions and dashed on. A few leaps of his horse brought him to the by-road where he was confronted by three mounted rebels who gave him such a warm reception that he wheeled in dismay and made for the brush on the right, in which he escaped without injury.

The exultant rebels, firing and yelling at the top of their bent, plunged into sight in pursuit of the fugitive; and as they did so I leveled my revolver at the foremost one and fired. I missed the rebel, but struck his horse in the side, bringing him to the ground and his rider with him. Meantime the other Confederates were moving into the highway ahead, and were now doing their best to escape from any more volleys from my pistol. Heedless of results, I leaped my horse over the fallen steed and his embarrassed rider and rushed after the fleeing enemy, firing as I went, though my aim could not, under the circumstances, be as effective as I could desire. A second horse was shot, and I saw the blood spouting from the wound. The man who rode this horse was, as was afterward ascertained, a doctor. Finding that my horse was too fleet for him he adopted the policy of conciliation; and as I was riding abreast of him to gain a shot at the third and last Confederate, who was in advance, he very politely remarked, "Hello, stranger, will you take a drink?" While speaking he offered his bottle in the most tempting manner. "No, sir," I said, passing on in full pursuit of the other rebel, who had managed to shoot five times at me without injury. I pursued him, however, to the creek, where, having emptied my revolver I stopped to reload it, while a guide from Harrison's force, who came up opportunely, held my horse. Other scouts had also put in an appearance, as Harrison approached; and the doctor, along with the rebel whose horse had fallen under him, was captured without resistance.

Having reloaded my pistol I started in company with the guide to ascend the hill on which the rebels were posted. The fact is, that at the very time in which we were making this perilous ascent, Col. Newsome had organized an ambuscade on both sides of the road, his lines stretching across it. We were not conscious of the imminence of the danger until we were within a few rods of the enemy in full force. A tremendous fire was opened upon us at once. I wheeled my horse into the road, sending two balls as I did so into the rebel ranks. Strange to say, neither the guide nor myself was struck by the enemy's volley. My companion was mounted on a swift horse, and aware we had no show except in flight, he suddenly exclaimed:

"Bill, I must leave you!"

The next instant he was thundering down the hill, out of range, leaving me to my fate. I was surely in a hot place, but the brush near by was my salvation. I plunged into it and kept on in a reckless and irregular way, until my horse came in collision with a fallen tree. The concussion was so violent that I was thrown over his head, falling some distance beyond, scratched and bruised but not dangerously hurt. While I was passing through these adventures the two opposing commands fought out their fight, and the enemy fled, after a brief but warm struggle, leaving the victory to us. I arose from the ground and, circling around in the woods afoot, struck the highway at a point where I was met by Col. Harrison, whose horse had been shot under him in the battle.

Two Union scouts, named Griffith and Mulharen, were down the hill some distance at the time I fired the two shots into the rebel ranks: Griffith said to the other: "Bill is in trouble again. Let us go up and help him out."

The will of these friends was good to help me out of my difficulty, and they rushed headlong up the hill. At this moment the rebels were in full career, sweeping down the eminence. Mulharen, who was mounted on a mule, was overborne by the tide of battle and was literally knocked over the fence, where he lay concealed until the conclusion of the fight. Meanwhile the mule, sadly demoralized, but not really hurt, scampered away to more desirable scenes. Griffith succeeded in getting away with two buckshot in his leg and thirteen in his horse.

# CHAPTER IV.

#### ADVENTURES AROUND FLORENCE.

Stop with Citizen—My Fellow Scouts—Capture of Seven Rangers—Our Captured Steeds—Servants in the Field—Angry Planter—Blackberry Cordial—Thrilling Charge—My Horse Killed—Miraculous Escape—Night Ambuscade.

Col. Cornine, of the Tenth Missouri cavalry, was directed by Gen. Dodge to take a command and inflict punishment on the rebels by burning all their factories at Florence, Alabama. I started in advance of this expedition and remained the first night with a citizen, who lived some miles away in the country. Next morning I was joined by two scouts, Tim Foley, of Davenport, and Isaac Harbaugh, of company I, of Iowa Second. We were all mounted, and when the colonel's command came up we started off to gather up stragglers and collect such intelligence as would be needed to assure success in this raid through the enemy's country.

We rode on until the sun was some hours past the meridian. There was a fine ridge which could be observed ahead of us. Before reaching it we noted a trail which had been made by passing horses. We followed it along the ridge until after night-fall, when we enquired of a citizen at his house if he had seen any one passing. Being answered in the negative, we continued on, reaching in a short time another residence, which could be seen in the obscurity. Here we silently and cautiously dismounted and fastened our horses in a place of concealment. Two buildings were observed near us. The one to our left was evidently the main building, while the other to the right was some sort of subordinate appendage.

To the best of my recollection, it was now within an hour or two of midnight. I was leading our party and we were all making for the main building, which loomed up before us, with no light streaming from the windows, when my attention was arrested by a sound of whispering voices, which came from the smaller structure near by. No light was visible, and as the noise I heard was suspicious and significant, I whispered to my companions to come to me and await developments. I then walked straight to the building from which the suppressed voices issued and gave the door a resounding kick, calling on the inmates at the same time to surrender, for they were surrounded on all sides by the Yanks, a thousand strong, who would shoot them down like dogs if they attempted to resist. My first summons brought no response, but the second one, enforced as it was by a more violent kick and by more impressive and threatening language, caused an excited voice from the interior to say:

"Wait till we get a light and then we will surrender!"

To this harmless request I, of course, consented, and while the inmates were procuring a light and opening the door I improved the occasion by directing my large troupe of imaginary Yankees to post themselves at convenient places and shoot down every man who sought to leave the house in any unauthorized manner. It was fortunate for us that the darkness was dense and profound, otherwise my little ruse might have been betrayed.

The moment the door was opened Foley and Harbaugh went in at my command to disarm the enemy while I remained outside, renewing my orders to the boys in blue, whom my fancy had conjured up for this emergency. In that old log building seven Texas rangers, all of whom were hard and disciplined fighters, had taken up their unsuspicious lodgings for the night. They were all, perhaps, seeking the arms of Morpheus when the awful call to surrender disturbed their ears. They were completely cowed, and, without a solitary show of resistance, they yielded themselves as prisoners of war. They were well armed and equipped, some of them having as many as three revolvers to the man. After the rebels had been disarmed they were bidden to remain where they were; the door was shut and we held them fast till morning, when our company overtook us, to whom our prisoners were transferred for safe-keeping. No pen on earth can describe the mortification of these fellows when they discovered, in the light of the glowing dawn, that they had been captured by three Yankees, instead of a thousand, as they had believed.

My next move was to visit the stable, followed by my two associates of the night. Here the first horse I saw I selected for my own; he was a blooded racer, possessing great speed and endurance. To him I transferred my bridle and saddle and was ready again for the road. Foley took from the stable a Canadian horse, with long, black mane and tail, and Harbaugh selected an iron-grey. My racer was somewhat fractious and skittish, but I held him in hand with ease, hoping for a chance to occur to try his fleetness.

The same morning, after starting on another scout ahead of the troops, we picked up four additional rebels, whom we turned over to Col. Cornine when his detachment arrived. I then rode off alone on my new racer, anxious to serve my country in some fresh exploit. I proceeded on, like Don Quixote, in search of adventures, until I came to a plantation, where some twelve or fifteen colored men and women were working in a field. At the moment I first observed them they were taking a temporary rest, sitting around in various places, according to their mood. They were greatly astonished when I opened the fence at a certain point and directed them all to go at once to it. They all obeyed, except two men, who started toward the house with all speed, entirely disregarding my command. To bring them to terms without any personal injury to them, I fired three shots in the air. This had the desired effect. The two men, fearful that their lives would be sacrificed if they did not obey, wheeled about and made for the gap indicated on a dead run. By this time the troops had neared us. Having heard the firing and not exactly knowing the cause, they formed a line of battle, but being undeceived in a short time, they came up to receive the colored deputation under my lead. All of the men and most of the women chose to go with the detachment rather than return to their master, and their choice was respected.

Having disposed of this matter, Foley, Harbaugh, and another scout named Derbin, accompanied me a quarter of a mile down to the mansion of the planter, who had just been bereft of his chattels. He was out in front of his house approaching us as we rode up. He was evidently in no amiable mood. He inquired with much excitement what we meant by taking his property without leave or license.

"We Yanks," I answered, dismounting and fastening my horse, "are going to take this entire country; and you may as well make your mind up to that, for it is going to be done."

Some further parley ensued which need not be reported, after which my fellow scouts and myself passed into the house, where, on a tour of investigation, we found a quantity of blackberry cordial, with enough of alcoholic stimulation in it to make one's head whirl. We tested its merits; and thus being fortified and prepared for fresh achievements we returned to our steeds and scampered away in the direction of Florence.

We rode on rapidly until we overtook the command, whose progress had been interrupted by the rebels in force. The latter were stationed on an eminence; and their position and numbers were so indefinite, their movements being covered, to a great extent, by the thick brush, that Col. Cornine made a solemn pause before ordering any dangerous assault. At this juncture we entered on the scene; and having been permitted by the commander to charge the rebels, we did so in good style. It was a rash act on our part, but we were stimulated by glory and blackberry cordial, and cared nothing for consequences. We were just reaching the summit, so as to gain a view of the rebel position, when a volley was fired into us which seemed to shake the very earth. Strange to say not one of us was injured. My three brethren, finding the place too hot for them, turned and fled, but my Dutch courage was up, and I dashed on toward the rebel lines, yelling and firing as I went. Meantime the enemy ceased firing, as they hoped to capture me without trouble. I was within a few rods of the muzzles of their muskets, when a full comprehension of my deadly peril almost turned me sick. I wheeled my gallant steed toward the brush; and as I did so, another broadside of musketry was leveled at me, which sundered the twigs around and sent the leaves whirling to the ground. This last volley was fatal to my poor horse; and he fell under me, perforated with three balls.

Never in my life had I been in so critical a position—so near death's door. I leaped from the fallen body of the steed and darted away into the brush, escaping from rebel bullets as by a miracle. I then circled round through the forest, emerging at last in a field where our cavalry took me at first to be a rebel. Undeceiving them they informed me that my fellow scouts were in the rear. I hastened to find them, but failed. It was now after night, and as I was returning towards Florence, the country being new and strange to me, I became somewhat bewildered. I proceeded on to the town, finding no one whom I knew, until I happened, by accident, to meet some members of the Tenth Missouri cavalry. Here I learned, for the first time, that the enemy had evacuated Florence, and our forces had taken possession. I found also a soldier who knew my horse, and knew, too, the exact spot where he fell. The soldier went with me to the place, where, having recovered my saddle and bridle, and ascertained, too, where the balls had struck my poor racer, we returned to Florence.

As our command could not hope to hold the town while it was surrounded on all sides by rebel troops, Col. Cornine moved out the same night. The four scouts, including myself, of whom I have spoken in this chapter, took up our line of march in advance. Before leaving the place, in the direction we were to take, we were obliged to cross a bridge on the farther side of which a number of rebels lay in ambush. We were in the act of passing over the bridge when the unseen foe opened out on us a deadly fire. The Canadian horse of Tim Foley fell dead, shot through the throat; and Harbaugh was wounded by a ball in the wrist. The ambushed rebels were shelled at once by our command and driven away. We then moved forward without further molestation. So in the summary of the affair two of the gallant steeds captured from the Texan rangers had bitten the dust in that day's encounter. Conversing afterward with the Texan who had owned the captured racer, he spoke in the highest terms of the steed's superior fleetness and value; but finally expressed his joy, as the Yankees had confiscated the animal, that he had been killed.

# CHAPTER V.

### THREE EXPEDITIONS.

Hensal—We Go to Ripley—Stop in Suburbs—Skirmish at Hotel—Capture Three Rebels—Drive Two Rebel Companies—Capture Town—Visit Des Moines—Back to War—Capture Job, the Guerilla—Capt. Stinnett's Guerillas—Strategy by Moonlight—A Jolly Prisoner Captured—Seizure of Horses.

HAVING learned that a large Confederate force was encamped somewhere in the vicinity of Ripley, several regiments were sent forward from Corinth to that particular section. I was sent on in front to make a scouting reconnoisance. James Hensal, of the Seventh Kansas volunteers, was detailed as my associate. He was a small man, but active and brave as a lion, and his hard service with Jennison, and Jim Lane's far-famed jay-hawkers, had fitted him for any post of severe duty to which he might be assigned. He is now living in Guthrie county, Iowa, in domestic quietude, cultivating a large farm.

We were both well mounted and in good condition for the road. We rode on continuously until we reached the suburbs of Ripley, a town of no very great importance. We halted at a house, dismounted and went in. The first person we saw was an old gentleman seated in a chair in an indolent or suffering attitude, while a colored boy, with brush in hand, was rubbing down his lower limbs. There was something in this which excited Hensal's merriment, and he began to ply the old Southron with seemingly grave but ironical questions.

"What is the matter, my friend," said he; "have you got the rheumatism, or is it the gout that is giving you a twitch?"

"Boy is rubbing me for my case," was the reply. Just then the spirit of mischief seemed to seize Hensal. He drew his revolver in the veriest bravado and flourished it around as though he was going to exterminate everyone within his reach. The terrified boy blanched almost to whiteness, dropped his brush and with a frightened howl, he fled from the room, tumbling heels over head in his rapid exit. For a moment the old citizen was in the direst consternation, fearing that his life would be sacrificed to the fury of this strange assailant. He was stunned by the epithets employed against him, one of which was, and it was a great falsehood, too, that he was disloyal to the South. At length order was restored, and while Hensal was ordering dinner and conversing with one of the women about the house, I took a stroll up town, feeling somewhat ill at ease at the events which had just taken place.

I sauntered leisurely along the street until I came in front of the hotel in the central part of the town. Here I met a citizen with whom I paused to hold a conversation. There were several listeners near by, and as I was a total stranger in the region, though wearing the Confederate garb, I felt assured that I had become an object of suspicion. This thought, together with the fact, perhaps, that the demon of mischief belonging to my friend Hensal had been communicated to me, impelled me to a rash and precipitate act. I was standing with one foot a little elevated when the suspicious circumstances around me began to excite my apprehension, and a remark made by the citizen brought the affair to a crisis.

Suddenly, without any premonition, I drew two revolvers from their concealment, and holding one in each hand, commenced firing with remarkable energy, sending the citizen and all other visible listeners to cover. They fled like so many deer started up by the hunters; meanwhile Hensal had just seated himself at the table in the house where our dinner was ordered. He was so intent on satisfying his hunger he did not hear the first shot; but on its frequent repetition his attention was directed to it in a manner so decided that he leaped from his chair, ran out of the house, led forth the horses, one of which he mounted, and hurried to my assistance.

Firing had ceased when he came up, and it seemed we had undisputed possession of the town. Hensal looked grave.

"Bill, you have got us into a scrape, hav'nt you?"

"No: I guess not," I answered; but to tell the truth, I felt quite anxious about consequences. The only way to do, however, was to carry out the programme as we had commenced it—that is, rashly and fearlessly. Leaving the horses for a brief time we rushed into the hotel, with every demonstration of fury, and captured two Confederate soldiers, who had fled thither for refuge. We managed to catch another one outside, and then having executed this exploit, we carried our prisoners to the building in the suburbs where we had first stopped.

On the day that these scenes were in progress two companies of rebel soldiers were encamped in the neighborborhood of Ripley. So near were they, indeed, that the explosion of my revolver could be heard. Believing that the Yankees were paying a visit to the place their officers ordered them out on double-quick to meet and chastise the cruel invaders. Having some decided intimation of their approach, and resolving to give them a lesson they would not soon forget, we left our three prisoners at the house in the suburbs, informing the owner that we would hold him responsible for their safe-keeping, and stating, also, that if on our return we should fail to find them, we would burn the house over their heads. Much of this was said, doubtless, in bravado, for we hardly had the heart to execute a threat so cruel and vindictive; but the owner accepted it all in dead earnest, and the prisoners declared that their respect for the old citizen and his property would hold them in confinement until we came to take them away.

Having thus disposed of our captives we left the house, remounted our horses and rode with the utmost speed through the village in the direction of the coming Confederates, yelling and firing promiscuously as we rushed past the houses. It so happened that the dust lay to the depth of several inches in the road, and the feet of our horses, as they swiftly sped along, kicked up a cloud of sand and dirt which made all objects in the rear of us, and around us, totally invisible. This dense eclipse, added to the frequent detonations of our revolvers, had the effect to make the approaching enemy believe that they were about to be gobbled up by an army of Yankees a thousand strong, or more. A panic seized them, and instead of advancing on us to give us battle, they wheeled about and fled in fatal confusion.

We pursued them half a mile beyond the limits of the village; then returning in triumph to find our three prisoners where we left them, we chartered a vehicle and conveyed them at once to our command, which was, at the time, about nine miles distant. Thus in that eventful day two Union scouts, without any assistance, except that which nature and our weapons gave us, captured three prisoners, routed two companies of rebels, and held possession of a Confederate town for at least two hours. That was glory enough for one day.   *   *   *

It was about this time that I went north to Alton with a prisoner, and being so near home I came up to Des Moines, intending to remain some time. Meeting U. S. Marshal Hoxie he told me I might extend my stay as long as I desired; but at the end of three days and a half time grew so irksome and monotonous with me I determined to return immediately to Dixie. Life in the service had become very attractive, and I proceeded again with all diligence to the army.

At the time of which I write the rebels had become very insolent and aggressive in the neighborhood of Corinth. One of our scouts, a soldier from Alabama, was fatally wounded within a short distance from our pickets. On another occasion a bold desperado by the name of Job, who had been raised in that section, passed into Corinth in the night and attacked one of our cotton-buyers, whom he robbed of $700, the bills being all of them of the denomination of two dollars. A heavy rain fell that night, making it impossible for the robber to get away from the vicinity without leaving very observable traces.

Next morning a number of us started in pursuit. It was not long before we noticed the track of a horse in close proximity to that of a mule. I told Harrison, chief of scouts, who was with us, that if he would give me a man to go with me I would capture the fellow or fellows who had made these tracks. The proposition was agreed to and my old friend Griffith, whose name has appeared before in these pages, was deputed to join me in the chase. We hastened on until we came to a point where the mule tracks diverged, going another way, while those of the horse went straight on. We followed the latter, and coming to the brow of the hill we saw, before making the descent, a house ahead of us and some distance to the left. I was mounted on a swift horse which had acquired quite an extensive experience in scouting. He was usually placid and tractable, but on occasions, especially when a house, as was the case here, or a fleeing rebel was in the perspective, he would start off on an impetuous gallop, with mane and tail flying out on the wind, and neither the voice of his rider nor the tension of the bit in his mouth could restrain his mad career. Off for the house on the left, which was his objective point, he plunged, leaving Griffith far behind in the race.

Before reaching the dwelling I observed the door to open a little ways and a man's face and head were seen furtively protruding, but in an instant they were withdrawn and the door was quickly closed. On sped my horse without pause or interruption until he stopped in front of the house as suddenly as though he had been shot through the heart. I made an effort to leap to the ground, but the momentum with which I had been moving, combined with the sudden halt, made my transfer to the earth more a tumble than a volunteer leap. In the hurry and crash of the descent the muzzle of my double-barreled gun struck the ground, forcing a quantity of sand and dirt into both chambers.

Deeming that this was no time to stop for trifles,

and being unconscious, too of the dangerous condition of my gun, I left my horse and ran with all speed around to the rear of the building, hoping to intercept any one who might be escaping in this direction. In a thicket near by a horse was standing with a man at his head, who was jerking, with every symptom of haste and cowardly fear, at the halter with which the animal was tied. My gun was instantly leveled at him, and at the same time I called out to him in a stern and authoritative manner:

"Hold up your hands and come here, sir, or I'll blow your head off!" The man was obedient. He desisted at once in his effort to get away and came to me very submissively. While disarming him I noticed in a roundabout which he wore the evidence that he carried something of value, perhaps, in the side-pocket. I turned it out and to my great joy a roll of greenbacks, together with a lot of bills on Southern banks, was developed to view. The greenbacks proved to be of the value of two dollars each, amounting in all to $198. It was manifest to my mind that this was a part of the $700 of which the cotton-buyer had been robbed. I had then captured the famous guerrilla, Job, who had committed so many depredations in that section. By the time the fellow was disarmed Griffith came up, somewhat mortified that the tardiness of his steed kept him from participating in this important arrest. He was a brave, good man, never shirking his post of duty in any emergency.

When we returned to Corinth with our captive it was ascertained that the other scouts had found and taken the mule whose tracks we had seen, but the rider, if there was a rider in the case, escaped unharmed. When Job was taken before our officer I was bidden by him to mount the prisoner barebacked on the mule and conduct him to a hollow not far away. I was also directed to bring the animal back; the plain inference was that the guerrilla was to be executed, as an example to all such villains. Never in the world did any other man p'ead more abjectly for his life than did this wretched ruffian. He groveled like a worm in his agony until the officer, who had been indulging in a bit of humor at his expense, commuted the sentence to something less harsh and melancholy. \* \* \* \* \*

At one time Harrison was sent with his regiment to the village of Lexington, West Tennessee, to measure out military justice to a certain Captain Stinnett, who, with a band of fifteen or twenty guerrillas, was making himself a terror in that part of the country. The village was his ordinary place of rendezvous; for his father-in-law resided there, running a hotel. I went with the expedition, and we arrived at our destination after night. It was arranged by Col. Harrison, as a part of his strategic plan, that while a large portion of his men should attack the town on one side, Griffith and myself should post ourselves on an eminence beyond a glen or a hollow to capture any fugitives who might be escaping in that quarter.

It is well to remark here that I bestrode a white horse; and it so happened, as the sequel will show, that a member of Stinnett's band owned a steed of the same color. The moon was shining rather obscurely; for it was veiled, most of the time, by fleecy clouds which swept rapidly across the sky. There was something spectral in our appearance, as we remained motionless on the hill, the effect of the tableau being heightened by the ghostly look of the animal that had carried me on this scout. All at once, as we were looking out from our post of duty, the general attack commenced; and we were surprised, in a short time, to see a rebel, with gun in hand, emerge from the hollow where he had hidden himself to avert certain capture. The manner of his approach to us proved that he was completely deceived in reference to our real character. He believed that we were Confederates like himself; and the style of our dress, as well as the color of my horse, fully justified this conclusion. He was evidently one of Stinnett's myrmidons, and seemed very eager to get away from the murderous Yankees.

"Where are the boys?" he anxiously inquired, as he was coming up. This question, so important to him, was repeated two or three times.

"Come here," said I, from my place in the gloom, humoring as best as I could the bald deception under which he was laboring. Wholly unsuspicious he came on until he was within two feet of me, when sudden as a flash the muzzle of my pistol was placed close to his head. At the same moment I said: "Drop that gun, sir, or I'll blow your brains out!"

Instantly the poor fellow saw he was sold. He had unwittingly given himself away to his enemies when he fancied himself among friends. The gun dropped from his nerveless grasp and he cowered in abject submission. I ordered Griffith to cover him with his revolver while I searched and disarmed the prisoner. After his scare was over he was discovered to be one of the jolliest souls in existence, making himself and his captors merry while talking about the Yankee deception which had been so successfully practiced by us at his expense. We captured our man, and held him, while the boys under Harrison who besieged the town, had succeeded in gobbling up a fine assortment of Capt. Stinnett's horses, but not a rebel was arrested, except the one in our possession.

# CHAPTER VI.

### FOUR EXPEDITIONS.

War-widows at Sugar Creek—The Out-building—The Dark Night—Rebel Horsemen—Capture of Five Rebel Officers by Strategy—Their Mortification—Captain Hamm—The Bridge at Night—The Surprise—The Leap for Life—Lost in the Swamp—Escape—Capture of a Spy—Rebel Retaliation—Price on Hensal's Head—Brown's Treachery—Keeping the Appointment—Brown Outwitted—Union Women—In the Hands of the Rebels—Death Stares me in the Face—Charge of Union Troops—My Deliverance.

GENERAL DODGE found it convenient to change headquarters from Corinth, Mississippi, to Pulaski, Tennessee. I was sent with Hensal from the latter place to learn all that could be ascertained in relation to a Confederate force reported to have crossed the Tennesssee River at or near Lamb's Ferry, some thirty-five miles from Pulaski. We made the trip without finding what we sought, for no rebel troops were seen in that vicinity. Returning, we arrived at Sugar Creek, fifteen miles from headquarters, after night-fall. At this point we rode up to a dwelling, which was inhabited, as we learned a little later, by two Confederate war-widows, and their children. Here we had permission to put up for the night.

After caring for our horses and partaking of supper we were directed to an out-building, a short distance from the residence, where we were to lodge until morning. It was a dark night, and very cold, too, for the season and the latitude. We fastened the door and then building a fire I sat down to enjoy it, while Hensal, who was weary and inclined to slumber, retired to rest. I was morbidly watchful and alert, feeling, for some mysterious reason, I had need of all the vigilance that could be summoned to my aid.

I was still sitting at the fire enjoying the warmth as it was communicated to my chilled frame, when my quick hearing caught the sound of horses' feet approaching the house. Soon after a party of men were heard to dismount and enter the building where the families resided. Cautiously I left my seat, went to Hensal and aroused him, saying in a whisper, "the rebels are after us." My companion started up in a hurry; and then after making due preparation we silently unfastened the door and proceeded out in the dense darkness on a tour of investigation. Stealthily we stepped to a window of the dwelling, from which a pane had been broken out, and through which a sickly light was gleaming from an antiquated saucer lamp. From our post of observation we saw, with more or less distinctness, five Confederate officers, all of them being commissioned, as the symbols they wore indicated. They were seated around the room, seemingly delighted to find a temporary refuge from the cold and darkness.

Having seen all we desired, and much more than we had bargained for, we retired from the window to hold a brief consultation. It was agreed between us that Hensal should proceed to the front door, and I should return to the window. Our object was to capture, by stratagem, this whole rebel delegation. We posted ourselves according to arrangement and waited for a favorable opportunity to execute our plan. By accident the door was a little ajar; and one of the women, standing near it, caught a glimpse of my friend on the outside. The silent start she made was not observed by any one; for an officer, just at the time, attracted attention to himself by remarking, "this is a very cold night, indeed."

The time had now come for action;. and the voice of Hensal rang out on the night like the blast of a trumpet—

"Come out here and I'll make it d--d hot for you."

The officers, taken thus by storm, started up in dismay and moved backward from the door toward the window through which I was gazing. It was my time now to address the beleaguered garrison—

"Confound you, " I exclaimed, "I'll make it hot for you *here*."

This was the nearest approach to profanity I ever made in my scouting experience. Simultaneously, or as nearly so as the nature of the case permitted, we commanded every man in the room to hold up his hands or suffer death; and while they all did so with alacrity we issued our orders to an imaginary troop of Union soldiers around us, assigning to different ones their part of duty in this emergency. As nothing could be seen on the exterior, owing to the profound darkness, our ruse had the desired effect. The enemy believed that the house was surrounded on all sides by a formidable Yankee host, and they felt that resistance was useless. Hensal at the door ordered them to come out one at a time; and the first one who approached was met by an authoritative command to stand aside in silence, while I, who meantime had retired from the window, disarmed him of all deadly weapons. One after another of these rebel dignitaries came out to give themselves up unconditionally; and when the last man had passed through the mortifying ordeal we conducted the whole five to the building where we had designed to sleep during the night. There we fastened them in, while we remained outside to watch.

It was not until morning that the officers, or the ladies, discovered that the important capture had been accomplished alone through the personal agency of two Union soldiers. The humiliation of the men was bitter and intense; and it was diminished in no respect, when, under cover of our revolvers, we compelled them to mount their horses and take the road in front of us to Pulaski, where we turned them over to the proper authorities. A sorry, crest-fallen set they were, who never forgot the bitter lesson which was taught them on this occasion.

\* \* \* \* \* \* \* \* \*

At another time as I was journeying alone on horseback between Sugar Creek and Lamb's Ferry, on the Tennessee River, I happened to meet a large, portly looking Confederate who, as I learned directly afterward, was a rebel sergeant. As my appearance indicated that I belonged also to the Southern army we entered at once into a friendly and confidential conversation. I affirmed, without any suspicion on his part, that I belonged to Forest's command; while on the other hand, he informed me he was an officer in one of Bragg's regiments, and had left the army of that general only three days before our meeting. Becoming more intimate and cordial in his communications he told me also that a large rebel force, under Longstreet, had just crossed the river at Louden, forty-five miles above Chattanooga, and was heading for Knoxville, which place he designed to attack.

After gaining all the information I possibly could, in

relation to the strength, situation and designs of the rebel forces in that region, I permitted the conversation to drift into other channels. The sergeant stated that four other soldiers had traveled with him from the army, and that they were stopping with friends not far away. He observed likewise that he was acquainted with a gentleman named Carter, of Southern sympathies, whose residence was in a neighborhood about seven miles from Pulaski. He stated that he and his friends were in great need of clothing; and he believed that Carter could be induced to go to Pulaski and smuggle from the Unionists the very articles of raiment which were necessary to supply common destitution. Of course, I was almost a total stranger in that part of the country, never in my life having seen the citizen to whom he referred; but I had a part to play, and as falsehoods, of the most unblushing character, are the capital in trade of the military spy, without which he is as helpless as an infant at the mercy of a crocodile, I was not slow in filling his mind with every sort and kind of deception which was deemed available. I averred that I knew Carter very well. I knew I could influence him to do all in his power to procure the desired clothing; and finally proposed to meet the sergeant and his comrades at the home of Carter on the following evening, at which time we would mature such plans as would serve our general interests. He took the bait with greediness and we parted in the most friendly manner.

I proceeded at once to headquarters and reported what I had learned to Gen. Dodge. I may remark here in passing that the intelligence I transmitted, in reference to the meditated invasion of Knoxville by Longstreet, turned out not only to be true as an episode in the history of the war, but in point of fact it was the first intimation of the proposed attack which had been received anywhere in the Union army. The reader will comprehend at a glance how valuable this news must have been to our general officers.

I then went to Hensal, who was chief of scouts, and reported. It was determined, on consultation, to capture the sergeant and his party. On the following day five of us, including the chief, mounted our horses and started away in the direction of Carter's residence. We rode on, until we arrived at a field, into which fresh tracks of horses, recently passing, were seen to diverge, taking the most direct course toward the house we were seeking. We continued on the main road; and after a little time we came to a creek, half a mile from our destination. Here, in a depression of the ground which concealed us from observation, three of us halted, while Hensal and another of our scouts whom we had given the nickname of "Biffle," proceeded on to the proposed rendezvous.

It chanced, as our two companions who had separated from us, rode up near the house they suddenly met the rebel sergeant who, with four others, confronted them from an opposite quarter. They all drew rein in the road; and as both parties were attired in Confederate gray it was not long before the most friendly relations were instituted. After the first salutations were over Hensal turned to the sergeant, who seemed to be the leader of his party, and made to him a startling revelation:

"My friends," said our chief with great apparent earnestness, "I know where, at this very moment, and not more than half-a-mile away, three or four Yankee soldiers have halted to feed their horses. Now, as there are seven of us, we have the best chance in the world to gobble up these fellows. If you will go with me I will take you to the spot at once."

"Lead on, comrade," responded the sergeant in his innocence of the deception practiced on him; "lead on, and we will follow to the death."

Off the united party started toward the creek, Hensal being in company with the rebels, while "Biffle" rode in the lead. Meanwhile we, who had remained behind, grew weary of our protracted vigil. It was already twilight; and I was apprehensive that our well-matured plans would fail. At last, really tired and disgusted with the whole proceeding, I led my horse up the acclivity near by to make a reconnoisance. In the gathering gloom I saw the party moving toward us; and soon the tramp of their steeds on the highway was distinctly heard. Mounting my horse and turning for a moment to my companions, I exclaimed in suppressed tones—

"My God, boys, they are coming!"

And come they did, with a rush, like that of a tornado in its wildest sweep. We formed in an instant and with a yell charged the advancing foe. An inequality in the ground, together with the dim obscurity, which began to settle on the scene, caused the steed ridden by our comrade, Norris, to fall, bringing the rider down with him, and excluding them both from any further participation in the fight. Thus reduced in strength we were outnumbered by the enemy; but Hensal, being assisted by "Biffle," Tim Foley and myself, succeeded in capturing two prisoners, one of whom was the sergeant. The last named individual, when he saw our chief turn against him with deadly weapons, and demand his instant surrender, was livid with astonishment and terror. He was the worst sold man on the continent, and so utterly demoralized, he cried out to Hensal, in piteous accents:

"For God's sake, don't let them kill me!"

He was answered that if he told all he knew concerning the illicit and contraband traffic which was carried on by Carter, in the interest of the Confederates, his life would be spared. He made the desired promise, and when he was turned over at Pulaski he made a statement, which led promptly to the banishment of the smuggler beyond the rebel lines. We had hoped, by our ruse, to capture the sergeant's entire party, but the accident to Norris, and the closing in of night, which rendered all objects somewhat confused, gave three of the fellows a chance to get away, of which they availed themselves in a hurry. \* \* \* \*

Before our general removal from Corinth to Pulaski I was directed to go down south into the interior of Mississippi, to notice the movements of a certain Captain Hamm, who, at the head of fifty rebel marauders, was playing, without restraint, the *role* of incendiary and murderer, at the expense of all Unionists. Returning from this quest on foot, after having made some discoveries which were useful to the loyal cause, I struck, after night, a corduroy bridge, which extended for some distance, not over any stream, but through one of those malarious swamps which are peculiar to the South. I had gone about one-third of the way across this rude structure when my attention was arrested by the tramp of horses' feet, which was distinctly heard in advance.

I listened intently and discovered that the party approaching, though from the darkness they were still invisible, consisted of several persons, all of whom were, doubtless, guerrillas in search of prey. It was a critical time for me, knowing well if I fell into the hands of these nocturnal butchers they would show me no mercy, especially if they ascertained my real character. I took my station at one side of the bridge, and the moment I caught a glimpse of their dusky outlines, aided as I was by a natural quickness of vision, which gave me a decided advantage in all enterprises in the dark, I leaped off, waist deep, into a hideous mixture of mud and water. If the splash I made was heard by the enemy, I knew it not, nor did I give them time to establish any effective pursuit. It was a cold, chilly night, and I floundered on in the Cimmerian gloom, through this wretched swamp, half frozen and covered from head to foot with muck and mire. Now and then, when I thought I had receded to a healthy distance from the bridge, I would clamber up to a resting place on one of the thousand elm roots which radiated in all direction through that wilderness of mud.

It was about a mile and a half from the place where I left the road to a railroad, which I intended to strike, and all the way to this point in question it was one universal morass, black as the bottom of a shaft at midnight, and gloomy as the grave. It has been stated hitherto that I was pretty well posted in wood-craft; that is, I could manage to find my way under very difficult circumstances, even in a strange country. On this occasion, however, as I was benumbed with cold, and compelled, also, to describe a somewhat devious path in my wanderings, I became confused and lost my way. It was hours before I emerged from the swamp, and then I hastened on until I reached the pickets belonging to our sharp-shooters, who were stationed a few miles south of

Corinth. To my great chagrin the vidette, who seemed to be repelled by my strange appearance, refused to permit me to pass in until morning, when my case would be properly reported to the officers. The result was I was forced to lie outside, on the cold, damp ground, without covering, and chilled to the marrow, until after daylight, when I was conducted inside the lines. \* \* \*

In one of his expeditions Hensal had the good fortune to recognize on the road and capture a famous Confederate spy named Johnson, on whose person were found some documents which proved to be a valuable prize to our own officers. It was a brave and prompt stratagem on the part of our chief, which placed the spy in fetters. The prisoner was duly tried by court-martial, was convicted, sentenced, and executed, refusing, with his latest breath, to save his life by making certain required revelations. He was game to the last; and his death, which was a great loss to the Southern cause, created quite an excitement in the rebel ranks. Retaliation was resorted to; and a reward of five hundred dollars was offered for the body, alive or dead, of the brave Union scout who had outwitted one of their most adroit and experienced detectives.

A young man, whom I shall call Brown, for his real name has escaped my remembrance, decided to earn the promised reward. He introduced himself to Hensal at Decatur; and in the course of a protracted interview he claimed that, although he belonged to a Southern family, and despite the fact, too, that he had a brother who was a rebel major, he had always been in sympathy with the Union cause, and no power on earth could divorce him from his loyalty to the old flag. Commonly, Hensal was quick to read motives, which had retired from the surface and lay deep down in the heart, masked by a veil of hypocrisy; but in this instance he was deceived, as subsequent events showed. The young man was a good actor, and was carrying out his plans with remarkable shrewdness and cunning.

At the time the interview took place, detailed above, I was at home in Iowa on a separate furlough. On my return to the South I went to Decatur, where Hensal gave me an introduction to the noble young Union friend, whose acquaintance he had happily formed. I glanced at Brown as we shook hands, and was struck at once by the suspicious peculiarity of his manner. He did not look me frankly in the face, but averted his eyes, casting them obliquely toward the floor. He was nervous and ill at ease, much like a man whose conscience or whose dinner did not agree with him. He professed to have important communications to make in reference to the Southern army and proposed, if Hensal would meet him on the Wednesday following, at a given hour, at a specified point on Flint River, seven miles south of Decatur, he would busy himself meanwhile to learn all he could concerning the plans and movements of the Confederates, and at the appointed time and place he would take great pleasure in transmitting valuable information to the scout. It is well to remark here that in working out his design he had made himself useful by frequently bringing rebel papers to Hensal, who gave him Union ones in return. He had played his cards well and was doubtless sure of winning the game. Hensal promised to meet him; and the interview being over Brown withdrew.

The moment after our young friend departed, or as soon at least as the sound of his footsteps died away, I turned to Hensal and told him he had been warming a viper in his bosom. I stated that the fellow carried the signs of deceit and treachery in his face and actions; and further, I expressed my surprise that a man who could read countenance as well as our chief of scouts could be deceived by the artifices of this boy. I warned him if he persisted in going to the appointment that it was his duty to take a force with him large enough to overcome all resistance. I was satisfied a conspiracy was on foot to capture Hensal; and after a time I succeeded in convincing him of the necessity of being prepared for any emergency. It was agreed then and there that seven of us should go to meet Brown; and if any hostile movement was attempted we would be in a condition to strike successfully.

On the following Wednesday I took six men and rode toward the rendezvous. Just before reaching the river we observed a high hill, while on both sides of the road a forest extended, broken in one spot by a clearing and dwelling, owned by a Union family named Deford. We proceeded on very cautiously until we came to the exact place of meeting; but Brown was nowhere visible. Just then my ears were saluted by a sound resembling the hooting of an owl, and so natural was it that my companions were deceived. I was suspicious, however, of every circumstance and keenly alive to the situation. I was certain that the sound we heard was a rebel signal of some sort, and was sure it meant mischief to us. I ordered Griffith, who was one of the party, to take a skiff which was moored near the shore, and cross to the other side, to institute an investigation. I then directed Foley to watch the progress of Griffith, and protect him from the shore with a revolving rifle. The other members of the party remained mounted, observing with great anxiety the skiff and its occupant, as they moved across the water. The experiment we had adopted might have cost us dear, for if an ambuscading party had been concealed in the brush on the opposite side, near the point at which Griffith emerged from the river, they might have slain him and then fled into the woods beyond pursuit. The general appearance in that quarter impressed me with the belief that if any large force of the enemy was posted in the vicinity it was yet too remote to do any mischief. We saw Griffith leave the boat and ascend the bank. The stream was not so wide as to prevent us from speaking to him and receiving answer. I enquired of him what he saw and learned that the fresh tracks of several horses were visible in the sand. While we were yet speaking we were startled by the sudden presence of young Brown on the other side, who issued from behind a tree, and walked toward Griffith. The scout regarded him suspiciously, and said sternly, as he leveled his weapon:

"I know you, sir, and if any harm befalls me while I am here you will be shot."

Brown was manifestly excited. He was not at the place of appointment, and I have no doubt, as the sequel appeared to demonstrate, that the signal came from him, calling his rebel friends in the woods to charge on us. Our numbers alone were our salvation. Brown made out at last to say:

"I'll be responsible for all that happens on this side of the river."

I was conscious that a rebel force was not far off, and at any moment we might be overwhelmed by superior numbers. I called on Griffith to return to the skiff and row back with all speed. He did so, leaving Brown to his disappointment. When we were all in the saddle again we turned back and ascended the hill. Before reached the house of the Unionist, noticed elsewhere, we met Mrs. Deford, swinging her sun-bonnet excitedly, and exclaiming:

"Get back, men! Get back, men! You are surrounded by a hundred rebels! Only this morning two of them came here and asked how many persons we had seen passing. I told them I did not know. You must get back, for the woods are alive with rebels!"

In her excitement the good woman exaggerated the number of our foes, but we were convinced that we had better get out of that part of the country. We spurred to the fence near the road, laid down the rails at the most convenient place, and plunged into a swamp, heading off our enemies by taking a circuitous route to Decatur. Arrived there we organized a company of twenty men, and returned to the river. At the ferry we learned that a band of fifteen rebels had recently crossed there, and we learned, also, that they would have attacked us if they had not been fearful of results. One place at least in which Hensal was expected to come held a Confederate, who designed to pick him off in passing. Our general officer was so indignant at the treachery of Brown that he ordered his soldiers to shoot him on sight, and burn the house in which he lived; but the vicissitudes of war, which soon took us away from Decatur, prevented the execution of this order. \* \* \*

Having heard that a large Confederate force had crossed the river at Eastport, I was sent in that direction to reconnoiter and gain desirable information. Returning from this excursion I stopped to water my horse in

Coldwater Creek. Just ahead of me was an eminence, on the summit of which I saw, with a start of surprise, for I had not heard their approach, a number of rebel troopers who rode down toward me like the rush of a whirlwind. As I afterward learned they were the vanguard of General Roddy's command; and when the detatchment moved into sight I knew they could not have numbered less than two hundred, all of them mounted and armed and eager for the fray with any inferior force. I was alone; and my first thought was to wheel and flee, relying on my usual good fortune to escape; but my horse was weary with long travel, and I was compelled to reject this suggestion which had come into my mind.

Why should I flee? There was no need of flight, so long as my butternut uniform, my long hair, and my perfect imitation of the Southern dialect could help me in this perilous crisis. Unless personally known to some of them, which was not at all likely, they could not prove that I was a Federal soldier. I made up my mind to remain where I was and risk the consequences. Without any appearance of agitation I waited in the creek until the head of the column reached me, when an officer rode up, who inspected me with great scrutiny and then began to ply his questions:

"Where do you belong, sir?" he inquired rather sternly.

I was prepared for this interrogatory, and responded with much promptitude—

"I am one of General Bragg's scouts, and am out now by his order on a mission of duty."

"Your statement, sir, may be true or false; that remains to be seen. You will go with us across the river, some twenty miles from here and when there you will have a chance to prove your identity."

My heart sank like lead; but I had so trained my nerves that there was no outward expression of feeling. Practically I was a prisoner for the first time in all my military experience. I knew, if confronted by the officers of Bragg's command that the declaration just made to my captors would be found to be untrue, and I would be hanged, or shot like a dog. Marching along with the column my mind was filled with gloomy forebodings; but my mental depression was not so great as to prevent me from thinking of some feasible scheme by which to effect my deliverance; for the resolution was strong in me to get away by some means before we crossed the fatal river.

I was riding on with my head bowed in melancholy thought, when all at once the two rear guards started forward and rushed past me, yelling like stentors—

"Yanks! Yanks! Yanks!"

This unexpected diversion threw the rebels into irretrevable confusion. They stampeded like a herd of frightened buffaloes, and all order was trampled under foot; chaos was come again. It seems that, at the most critical moment of my life thus far, a Union regiment of mounted infantry, led by Colonel Rowatt, of Illinois, had come up with a rush and charged the rear of the Confederate troops, driving the entire command before them like so many sheep pursued by devouring wolves. Some of the rebels were killed, while others were wounded, and sixty of them were captured. I was somewhat acquainted with Col. Rowatt; and taking the first opportunity which presented itself, in the midst of prevailing disorder, I made my way to him, reported myself and the situation in which I was placed; and having been duly recognized I felt that I was at liberty again, and ready once more to do service for my country. The whole period during which I was a captive did not exceed an hour and a half.

# CHAPTER VII.

### A THRILLING CHAPTER.

The Conscript Sergeant—Pursued by Guerrillas—Flight through the Woods—Lost in the Forest—The Baying of Blood-hounds—The Raft—Swimming for Life—Startling Strategy on the Road—Reach Savannah—Form a Union Company—Sleeping in the Woods—Five Guerrillas Killed—Rebel Vengeance—We Lodge in Courthouse—Invaded by Guerrillas—The Warning Cry—An Awful Leap—Murder of my Friends—Fleeing to the Brush—My Blistered Feet—Kind Union Friends—Hulse and Britton—We Cross the River—In the Brush—Blood-hounds again—Leaky Skiff—More Friends—Horses Bought—Headed Off—Wander in Forest all Night—Kirk's Guerrillas—Return to Pulaski.

In the spring of 1864 General Dodge was succeeded at Pulaski by General Stockweather. After the change was effected I was sent down into Mississippi on a general scouting expedition. On my return I chanced to meet a conscript officer in the rebel service. Entering into a friendly talk with him, as he did not suspect me, I obtained much valuable intelligence, which I designed to report to the proper authorities at the earliest moment. We finally separated and I rode on. When within five miles of the Tennessee River, as I was moving along at a moderate gait, unsuspicious of danger, seven or eight rebel guerrillas, well mounted, came on me with such a suddenness that I was really taken by surprise. The stern voice of their leader called out to me to "halt!"

but as I gazed into their brutal and vindictive faces, in which I saw no symbol of mercy or magnanimity, I determined to make a run for liberty and life. In fact, this was the only alternative, for guerrilla warfare was brutality and murder in their most atrocious forms. Thus resolved, I summoned all my energies, struck the spurs into my horse, and darted forward on the road, pursued by these human wolves, whose yells pierced my ears like noises from the infernal pit.

The race was kept up for a mile or so, when gazing backward I discovered, to my infinite chagrin, that the distance between myself and the enemy was rapidly diminishing, and I was aware that in a very short time the intervening gap between us would be closed if I did not resort to strategy to secure my safety. My resolution was taken, and at a favorable moment I leaped bodily from my steed, leaving him to pursue his riderless way. I struck lightly on my feet and plunged into the brush which lined the road. Away I went through the intricacies of the forest, circling around trees and scrambling through the bushes until I was satisfied that the man-hunters were foiled, and I could take time to rest. By this time it was growing dark and soon the great woods by which I was invested were enveloped in a mantle of blackness.

After resting awhile I struck out again for the river. I wandered for hours in the pathless forest, for the sky being clouded over there were no means at command to indicate the course that should be taken. It was, I knew, but a few miles to the river, but the time it took me to reach this temporary destination proved that I had been going blindly in a circle during the greater part of the night. Day was breaking when I caught sight of the broadly flowing stream, and I was about to congratulate myself on the success with which I had thus far eluded pursuit, when off in the distance behind me I heard the deep and ominous baying of blood-hounds. That I was the object of vigorous and persistent search on the part of the rebels whom I had baffled, seemed to admit of no reasonable doubt, and a thrill of involuntary terror passed through my frame. A fence was close at hand, and in the hurry of a quick resolve I took a number of rails and fastened them together with strips of bark, so as to form an improvised raft. It was a rude piece of mechanism, it is true, but it was the best that could be done in the dangerous emergency. By the time the work was completed and the frail craft was lying near shore, ready for the voyage across the river, the bay of the hounds was heard appallingly nearer and louder.

Not an instant now was to be lost. Placing my hat, revolver and shoes on the raft, I plunged into the water and swam, guiding the craft with one hand while with the other I propelled myself and the cargo in my possession. However expert in all common athletic exercises I may have been, I was not a very proficient swimmer, and hampered as I was by the raft, and by the swiftness of the current, I was soon exhautesd and well-nigh drowned. To save myself I took my hand from the raft, and while my earthly goods were swept away from sight, never to be restored to their owner, I employed the remnant of strength left to me in reaching the farther shore. I crossed at a point somewhere between Eastport and Savannah. I stepped in dripping clothes up the bank, and was moving off into the brush, with faltering step, for I was greatly fatigued, when on turning around I saw a couple of the hounds standing on the opposite shore, glaring at the fugitive who had escaped their jaws. If they attempted to swim the river in pursuit I knew it not, for their presence so near me stimulated my wasted energies to such an extent that I fled with all speed into the forest.

Some time elapsed when I emerged into a highway, on which I traveled some distance, keeping a cautious lookout each way for approaching enemies. The tramp of a horse's feet, striking the hard road not far away, fell on my ears, and looking in that direction I saw the outlines of a rider as he rose to the summit of a hill in advance. As yet he had not seen me, and my purpose being formed, I retired, hastily and silently, to the bushes, where I concealed myself. The horseman came on without any suspicion of danger, and when he neared my place of concealment I suddenly stepped out and approached him, with every appearance of fearful excitement.

"Did you see them Yanks down thar?" I enquired, in woful agitation.

"No: whar are they?" said he, alarmed beyond measure at what he saw and heard; for my uncouth appearance was enough in itself to startle the bravest beholder.

"Why, right down here," I replied, pointing to the bushes whence I had issued. "Confound them, they have stripped me, as you see, and left me nearly naked!" Whether the man I was addressing was a citizen or a soldier I never knew. His dress and manner, as well as his language, indicated nothing except that he was a full-blooded Southron. He was terribly frightened, and as I saw him sitting in stupid terror, and taking down the story of Yankee meanness I was reciting, I felt that the time for action had come. Leaping over five or six feet of space which lay between the rider and myself, I placed a firm grip on his shoulders, and before he was conscious of the real situation he was dragged headlong to the earth. Then, as I did not mean to kill him, I gave him two violent blows in the face with my clenched hand, leaving him insensible but not dead. It took but a brief time to despoil him of his hat, shoes and revolver, and having fully appropriated these articles to myself, the hat and shoes fitting very well, I sprang into the vacant saddle and was off like a shot.

It was about thirty miles to Savannah, and that was my destination. Without farther interruption I reached it at last. I stopped there for a time to cultivate an acquaintance with Union families in that vicinity and to concert plans to defend them against the aggressive insolence and brutality of surrounding rebels. Besides large forces of Confederates who were marching through the country, under the lead of Generals Biffle, Forest and others, leaving a track of desolation behind them, there were numerous bands of guerrillas, headed by such infamous wretches as Burt Hayes, Bob Danmon and Dock Smith, who never felt the emotion of pity or compassion. The sight of a genuine patriot made their eyes gleam with a glitter of deadly ferocity. They were tigers in all but outward seeming, often seeking their prey by night, and never tiring in their pursuit of blood.

While sojourning in Savannah I organized and headed for local defense a company of twenty-six men. We did effective service in hunting down guerrillas and in protecting loyal familes from rebel incursions. For weeks I remained out doors during the night, for when sleep was demanded I would seek, with my companions, some lonely lair in the neighboring forests, where the earth was our couch and the boughs and foliage of overshadowing trees and bushes were our covering. It was a life of peril and privation, but I was willing to share it in common with many Union men, whose homes and dear ones were close at hand, but who were forced to leave them to find security for their lives in the fastnesses of the great forest.

On one occasion an urgent message was sent to me from a settlement twenty miles away, requesting me to take a number of my men and assist the Unionists of that neighborhood in driving out the squads of desperadoes whose presence there had become intolerable. I consented to go, and taking three of my soldiers, Hulse, Britton and Swayne, we mounted our horses and rode off one evening toward the designated place. Five miles out we stopped till morning at the house of a Unionist. After breakfast we traveled on until the sun was approaching the meridian; we were then near the settlement to which the message had directed us. The tracks of five horses, freshly made, were detected in the road. Soon after this discovery was made we caught sight of a party of riders some distance in front. On each side of the way were dense woods, and as the party ahead were moving on with every appearance of careless confidence, we were certain they had not as yet seen us.

We observed a by-path which intersected the highway a few hundred yards in advance of the horsemen we were pursuing; and Swayne said:

"There is nothing to hinder us from going through the woods here to that path yonder; and then by moving on it down to the road again we can easily intercept them. One or two of our number should remain here to cut them off if they retreat this way."

The suggestion was a good one, and it was adopted. With cocked revolver, ready for action, I remained behind on guard, while the others rode off diagonally among the trees. They struck the path and kept within its narrow limits until they came to a place near the highway, where they dismounted, tied their horses and secreted themselves in the bushes. It is hardly necessary to state here that the men whose lives we sought were, from their general appearance and manner, guerrillas of the most brutal type. To rid the world of these monsters by any kind of warfare that could be employed was a duty which every good citizen owed to himself, to his family, and to his country.

At the instant the guerrilla party were passing the place of ambush they were fired on by the boys; and three rideless horses were seen rushing forward and snorting with fright along the road. Three of the men were slain outright; and the other two, taken thus by storm, as well as by strategy, attempted to escape. Now was the time for the part I had to take in this thrilling and bloody drama. Rushing forward and taking the best aim I could, the trigger was touched, and as the smoke from the discharge was drifting away among the trees the fourth man fell dead from his horse, having been shot through the heart. The last one, being nerved by desperation, aimed at me with his carbine and fired, the ball whistling very close to my head. I rode down on him, and just as we were moving side by side I caught him by the hair and attempted to drag him to the ground. His resistance was terrific, and for full fifty yards we kept on together in this way before I succeeded in bringing him down from the saddle. By this time my horse was in full career; and I found that to rein him up was impossible. I was compelled to quit the fallen guerrilla and take a free ride against my will. During my enforced absence, which did not last long, for I soon obtained control of the steed, my companions completed the bloody work in hand. The bodies of five men, who in life had been guilty of every possible atrocity, including rape and wholesale murder, lay stark and stiffening on the road; while their horses, bearing their vacant and gory saddles, fled away in wild affright.

The rebels in the neighborhood in which the event just recorded took place, were inspired with a wholesome dread of Yankee courage and Yankee cunning. The devil had been given a taste of his own fire and brimstone; and though it was not to his liking it made him more respectful in his demeanor toward his Union neighbors. We heard, however, after our return to Savannah that the enemy whom we had left greatly demoralized were kindling a blaze of fury, which was intended to consume my little company. For awhile their active hatred toward loyal men in their midst showed a wonderful abatement; but the fact is, they were preparing to strike us with all the force of their malignant vengeance. It was not long before the conflict came, the details whereof are as imperishable in remembrance as the mind itself.

It was our habit, as before stated, to pass our nights in the woods; but desiring a change in the character of our sleeping apartments, eight of us, all being members of the company, repaired one evening to the court-house in Savannah, and took up our lodgings for the night in an upper room. This whim of ours was simply a reckless invitation of danger; for while there we were liable, at any moment, to suffer an awful penalty for our rashness. We slept soundly; and at daylight next morning we were startled by a feminine voice repeating from the street these words of fearful warning—

"Biffle's men! Biffle's men! Biffle's men!"

It was a Union lady living in the town, as we subsequently learned, whose signal tones thus thrilled us like a blast from the trumpet of doom. We all started to our feet; and I stepped to an adjacent window to reconnoitre the menaced peril. The sun was hardly up, yet the broad light of day was on the world. Bestriding their horses on the main street, in full view, were two Confederates armed to the teeth; and in another direction close by was a large force of rebel troopers, drawn up near the jail in line of battle. I may as well pause here, to state what I learned at a later period, that the three guerrilla companies of Hays, Smith and Danmon, had been consolidated for this occasion, numbering in all thirty-five men. They had come to retaliate on us for the deaths we had caused in their infamous brotherhood.

The sight I saw from that window was enough to sicken me; but by a supreme effort of will I calmed my nerves and collected my energies to meet the crisis, with a steady hand and a cool, determined brain. I was lightly dressed, and this was all the better for me. My shoes were off; and the lower extremities of my pants were thrust inside the socks which encased my feet. I examined my revolver, which was the same I had taken, sometime before, from the rebel whom I dragged from his horse, just after I swam the Tennessee River. The weapon was rusty, and in very bad condition. Manipulate it as I might, it would not stand cocked; and with a gesture of disgust I returned it to its place and prepared to quit the room.

By this time the place where we slept was nearly deserted. I heard my comrades rushing down stairs to find prompt egress before escape was rendered impossible. Conscious that it was no time to tarry I followed them, and in point of fact there was but one behind me, when I emerged into the open air. Springing out from the building and glancing around I noticed, with an involuntary shudder, that the assailing party were within a few rods of me, charging, yelling and firing like so many fiends from the lowest pit. Though behind at the start, it was but a few moments before I had passed all my companions, some of whom spoke to me as I went by; but this was manifestly a case in which, as Hulse had remarked, when the alarm was given, "every man must take care of himself," and so I kept on. We were sadly outnumbered, and besides this, we were afoot, and in this contingency nothing but fleetness in the race could hope to win. For a hundred yards or so the ground descended in a gentle slope; at the end of this was a formidable fissure, or gully, excavated by the washing of many rains. As I afterward discovered, it was ten feet deep and fifteen wide. I was almost on its verge before I was aware of its proximity. The sight thrilled me with momentary terror, but knowing that certain death was behind, I summoned all my powers, and lifting myself into the air, with one mighty effort my feet were planted solid on the farther side. Pausing not an instant here, for the balls were whistling murderously all around, I fled on. Springing over a fence into a cornfield, I had measured half its length, when I heard a shout of fiendish exultation from the rebel crew. I knew what this meant and deplored it with feelings too strong for expression. That shout was the death-knell of my brave comrades.

From the field I plunged into the thick undergrowth of the Tennessee bottom, and was safe, for the time, from pursuit. It is fitting to record here, though I did not know it at the time, that but two of the eight who slept in the court-house were saved from a violent death—that is, Hulse and myself—six of the boys were murdered before they reached the gully, and their assassins gloated with shouts over their dying agonies. Hulse was run over in the charge, but by a miracle he was not greatly injured. Taking advantage of the general confusion he picked himself up when the rebels had passed beyond him, and striking out in a rearward direction he managed to get away.

The terrible race I have described had prostrated my energies, both of mind and body, to an extent that was absolutely fearful. My heels and toes were black with painful blood-blisters, caused by the obstructions and the hard, uneven ground over which I had recklessly rushed; yet I was not permitted to rest long in the brush where I halted, for I knew that the human blood-hounds, who had murdered my companions, and who had sworn to take my life, would not pause, day or night, in their sleepless pursuit, so long as a hope of ultimate success remained. So in a short time I regained my feet, aching in every limb, and moved wearily through the woods to the residence of a Union man, whose acquaintance had been previously formed. Here I was cordially welcomed, and the good wife, who was a tender and considerate nurse, bandaged up my sore feet and gave me a pair of old moccasins, which were of inestimable service. The friend with whom I stopped had no neighbors to share with him in his Union sentiments. What neighbors he had were rebels, who suspected him and watched him closely. If a stranger was seen about the house their impertinent curiosity would find vent in annoying questions and suspicions.

Under the circumstances it was deemed best, after my wounds were dressed and my appetite refreshed, that I should conceal myself among the weeds on the premises. This was done, and while all my wants were supplied by members of the household, my kind benefactor, in deference to a wish I expressed, mounted his horse and rode over to Savannah to ascertain the fate of my comrades. All that day I lay in the weeds, in a state of mental suspense, and bodily suffering beyond the ability of my pen to describe. In the evening my host returned, bringing with him two of my company, whom he had fortunately found. One of these was Hulse, whose narrow escape that morning has been recounted, and the other was a soldier named Britton, belonging to my decimated command. The latter was not one of the hapless eight who slept in the court-house.

That night, although I was not in a condition to travel, and Hulse was very little better, we bade farewell to our kind host and his family; and pushing out through the darkness we crossed the Tennessee River, and never halted until we reached a Union settlement, to which we had been directed. Here, under the guardianship of people who were poor but loyal, we remained concealed for a week, during which time our principal subsistance was boiled corn. Through all these days and nights of pain to me, and anxiety to all of us, there was truly a reign of terror in that part of Tennessee valley. All the roads and paths, and indeed all the avenues which offered the hope of escape to a Union fugitive were eagerly watched and guarded by rebel bands; and it seemed that nothing but the intervention of a miracle could save us from capture and death.

It was a long time before the bruises and blisters on my feet were healed. In spite of my condition it was deemed best, at the end of a week, for us to leave our friends and try again the uncertain chances of flight. We chartered an old skiff and embarked in it one night, designing to reach the Union lines at Johnsonville, many miles distant. We had proceeded about two miles when our leaky craft gave such evident signs of distress, we were obliged to touch the shore at once, and seek some means to repair our sinking boat. We were now on the Middle Tennessee side; and as we walked on, a light we had seen from the river directing us, we came at length to a dwelling where lived, as we soon discovered, an old colored man and his wife. The information we obtained here was of the most discouraging character. We were told that the rebels had been crossing the river, just below where they lived, all through the preceding day, keeping it up thus far in the night. We learned also that patrols were out in every direction, especially in the one in which we desired to escape. With a feeling of disappointment, impossible of description, we gave up the projected voyage, and asked our colored friend to describe the way to the nearest Union residence. He told us that half a mile away we would find the place we sought. Thanking him for his kindness, after receiving such suggestions as we needed to guide us on the way, we struck out through the black night and finally arrived at the house tired, weak, and despondent.

Another week of hiding in the brush followed, along with our customary diet of boiled corn. The awful monotony of those tedious hours, whether of darkness or of light, as we lay, or sat, or crawled among the bushes, will never be forgotten. It was broken at last by a rude shock. One night our ears were suddenly invaded by the curdling bay of blood-hounds, whose presence was not far removed from us. I had heard such sounds before, and knew what they meant. Our danger appeared imminent; we felt there was no time to lose. Issuing from our hiding place we again took up our weary and dispirited line of march, never stopping till we arrived at the home of a Union friend, about two miles from Savannah. Thus it will be seen that, after wandering around for many days, as our pitiless fate had decreed, we were back once more near the place from which we had started, bringing with us the chilling conviction that there was less prospect now than ever before of getting away in safety from the cordon of enemies investing us.

Several days passed away, during which our new Union friend, at the risk of his own life, kept us in a place of concealment; but this could not last long. Making preparation for the crisis we saw approaching, we gave our benefactor money enough to buy three horses and their equipments, along with such weapons as would be needed in a perilous journey. The purchases were made; and it was well for all concerned that such was the case, for one evening our friend came to us, excited even to weeping. He informed us that the rebels, or rather the guerrillas, were in force all around, scouting on all paths and roads, and murdering every Union man that came in their way. He stated that one of his neighbors was assassinated that very day, and he did not know how soon his own life would be demanded by these ruthless savages. He added that for our own safety, as well as for his, we must get away at once, though he knew we had a fearful gauntlet to run, and God only could foresee how it would all end.

We listened with grateful attention, for he had been very kind to us. Gladly would I record his name, and that of many others who gave me help in those days of trial, but a treacherous memory which recalls the incident, but not the name, is my apology for this omission. We accepted the counsel of our friend, and while the night was upon us, and the skies were overcast with clouds, down which lightning gleamed fitfully, we sprang on our horses and took down the main road toward Clifton, about twenty-five miles from Savannah. We traveled on through the gloom until we reached Indian Creek, near which was the home of a Unionist, with whom I was acquainted. Riding up to the house we were recognized by the wife and daughter, who came to the door, the former tearfully informing us that her husband and son, fearing for their lives if they remained, had started that day for the Union lines, with no very sanguine hope of reaching them. She added that just before we came the explosion of twelve guns was heard on the other side of the creek, directly in the course we intended to take. Thus, a lion was in our path, too formidable for us to encounter. We could not hesitate as to the proper route to take in this emergency, and after expressing our sympathy and bidding adieu to our weeping friends, we wheeled in the road and started off again toward the point from which we had come.

It was now some hours in the night, and the storm

which had been so threatening for some time before passed around without touching us. We arrived at length at a place where a path diverged to the left. I was somewhat acquainted with the geography of the country, and knew that the path before us led toward a small village called Old Town, but how remote it was, was simply a matter of conjecture. Forming a new resolve, I turned to the boys, who were a few paces behind, and said:

"Boys, it won't do for us to stay here. By some means or other we must get out of this country, and I propose to take this road to do it."

Britton and Hulse promptly assented, and still keeping the lead, followed closely by the others, I turned sharply into the interceding way and pushed on beneath the overhanging foliage, amid profound gloom of night, until, after a time, we came to a house, before which we stopped to make inquiries in regard to our route. It was a minute or more before our louder summons brought a response, and when it came it did not issue from the door, but from an opening in the window, from which a pane of glass had been broken out.

"What do you want?" the voice demanded, gruffly.

"We want to know," I answered, "how far is it to Old Town; and besides this, we wish you to give us, if you please, the proper course for us to take to get there."

"It is about two miles and a half," responded the voice; and then came a string of such crooked and ambiguous directions, as to the proposed route, that in sheer disgust we stopped the conversation and moved away from the house. On we went through the darkness, crossing a stream or two in our course; and after an indefinite period of time had elapsed we rode into a clearing, in the midst of which was a solitary house. In front of it stood two horses, with the equipments for riders, awaiting, as it seemed, the return of their owners from the dwelling.

It was not our purpose that night to provoke a conflict; for we were fugitives in the land of enemies, fleeing for our lives from torture and death. This being the case we moved on, with every possible precaution, beyond the house; and then, pushing on with more rapidity, we followed the path which lay obscurely before us until it became so dim as to be almost imperceptible. At last it faded out altogether, leaving us at midnight or later in an interminable forest, whose tremendous gloom enthralled and bewildered us. Already, as we knew, we had traveled many times over the distance to the village, the way to which we had inquired; and we were lost beyond all dispute. Still we urged our horses onward, among hills, trees, underbush, and ravines, in the desperate hope of finding our way out of this labyrinth of difficulties. On we wandered, up and down, and around in the grasp of varied entanglements, until, as morning approached, our attention was arrested by the tinkling of a cow-bell, mingled with the crowing of chickens. We were near some residence, that was evident; and pushing on we presently halted in front of a dwelling in the midst of cultivated premises. We summoned the inmates; and after a time a voice, strangely familiar, was heard issuing from a fractured place in the window. It was now broad daylight, so that we could perceive the voice came from an old citizen, whose face only was visible behind his breastwork. My first question was significant as follows—

"Did a party of three horsemen call here early in the night and inquire the way to Old Town?"

"Yes," was the reply.

So to our grief and humiliation it was clear we had halted at this very house hours before; after which we employed the greater part of the night in wandering about in a circle in the manner commonly adopted by those who are lost.

Nothing now remained to do but to obtain new directions and make a new start. These we did; and in the course of a half, or three-quarters of an hour, we reached the village we sought. On the streets, as we rode through, we observed the hoof-prints of many horses recently made. From our garb and appearance we attracted but little attention from the villagers. Beyond the town we accelerated our speed; and gaining the summit of a long hill we sprang to the ground and fastened our steeds. We then walked back a quarter of a mile, obliterating all the way the prints of our horses' feet, thus checkmating all pursuit as far as practicable.

Returning we mounted again, and abruptly left the road, turning into the woods at right angles, and moving off eastward. Despite the mistake which had been made the night before in regard to our course, it was true, nevertheless, that when the chances were not too strongly against me, I was rather expert in finding my way to a given destination, through a pathless country; and on the present occasion the talent of which I write was called into lively exercise. My object was to reach the home of a certain Union man whom I knew, and being acquainted with the general direction, we pushed on over ravines and through valleys, and over hills covered with trees and brush, until near noon we came to a creek, close to which was the place we were seeking. Arriving at a fence belonging to our Union friend we laid down a tier of rails, and passing through, the fence was reconstructed precisely as it was before we touched it. We then took the precaution to efface all the tracks made by our party from the point at which we diverged from the highway to a place inside the field, where we took saddle again and proceeded to a thicket not far off. Here we alighted and tied our horses. Leaving the boys I went up to the house, where a cordial reception awaited me. An arrangement was effected by which I was to return to the thicket and remain with my friends in concealment until dusk, when we were all to take supper at the house. Repairing again after supper to the bushes, we mounted and pursued our gloomy way through the darkness.

Twelve miles distant lived a loyal citizen named Arnold, to whose hospitality we had been commended. Wayworn and nearly exhausted from sleepless vigils, we rode up at last to the residence of our new friend. Here, too, we met a warm and inspiring welcome. A son of Mr. Arnold, who was a soldier in the Federal army, was at the time at home on furlough, but the poor fellow was doomed, like ourselves, to pass many tedious hours in the bush. In company with him we spent in the woods the entire day which succeeded our arrival. Meantime a little son of our host took my horse to a neighboring blacksmith-shop to be shod. When night came Mr. Arnold kindly conducted us to a Union settlement, from which we were guided still further on our way by two young men, who volunteered their services.

An exchange of horses was effected between a member of our party and one of these guides, and on the journey a proposition was made to test the speed of the newly acquired animals. It was accepted and off we all went with a rush, tearing along the road as though Satan himself was driving. Before we were aware of our danger we rode almost in collision with a number of horses stand-ing in front of a house by the wayside. Instantly several men who were in the building rushed to the door and peremptorily ordered us to halt, but as their numbers were too great for us, we wheeled like a flash and sped away, expecting every moment to hear the crack of pistols in our rear. The explosion, however, did not come, and we made our escape unharmed. We heard afterward that the party with whom we came thus in contact were Kirk Meyers' guerrillas, who were a band of despera-does infesting the country.

The two guides, whose kindness has been acknowl-edged, conducted us successfully to two Union neighbor-hoods. From the latter place a blacksmith guided us on still farther to the home of a patriot named Howser. This gentleman was hiding from the rebels in the woods when we rode up. A message was sent to him request-ing his presence at the house, but for a time he refused to obey it, suspecting that the rebels had invaded his premises. He came in at last, and consenting to accom-pany us, we pushed off again through the forest, and cir-cled around Lawrenceburg, being guided by Mr. Howser, who was on foot. It was his habit to keep some distance ahead and when he came to an intersecting path, or road, he would reconnoitre for a moment and finding the coast clear in all directions, would clap his hands as a signal for us to advance. In the course of a few hours we sep-arated from our guide and then made our way to Pu-laski.

Before closing this portion of my narrative I wish to

state that, some time after my return to Pulaski I happened by accident to be present while a Unionist, known as Major Howard, was speaking to a party of soldiers in reference to the murderous incident which took place, as described in these pages, at the court-house in Savannah. He stated that the leap which one of the escaping Unionists made over a wide ditch, was so much talked about as a marvel of activity, he took the trouble one day to measure the exact distance. He found it to be fifteen feet across and ten deep. At the close of his statement I had the pleasure to inform him that the feat was executed by myself.

# CHAPTER VIII.

#### THE TWO EXPEDITIONS.

Trestle-work—In the Rebel Lines—Brown's Corral—Fun with Colored Men—The Comic Flight—The Block-house—Dispatch to Morgan—Rebel Cavalry Scared from Rogersville by Midnight Ruse—Dispatch to Rosseau—Two Recruits—Start for Pulaski—Pray for Darkness—House on Hill—Rebel Ambush—Bishop's Capture—The Retreat—The Path and the Hill—The Hot Pursuit—The Mantrap—Scaling the Hill—The Night-watch—Tracks in the Road—On to Pulaski—Bishop and his Mother.

AFTER the rebel General Forrest, had taken Athens, I was dispatched to the trestle-work at Sulphur Springs to take a look at the situation. While still a mile away from this place I heard continuous firing, and knew that the Confederates were engaged in hostilities. Feeling confident from my disguise my real identity would not be suspected, I left the road and found my way into the rebel lines and mingled freely with rebel officers and men. I talked bitterly in reference to the North, and declared the time would soon come when we would take Pulaski and every other post wrested from us by Yankee invaders. I remained half an hour, gaining intelligence which afterward did good service to our cause, and having gratified my curiosity I took my leave.

I went at once to a noted place called Brown's Corral, where several thousand colored people were kept and fed at the expense of our government. I sought an interview with Brown, the commandant, and told him of the approach of Forest, advising him to use all diligence in getting his people away to Pulaski before the blow which threatened fell. My advice was immediately taken and the place was soon evacuated. Having done my duty here I rode off on my return to Pulaski. When about a mile on my way I observed a man of color, mounted on horseback, and wearing an old slouch hat, emerge from a path into the road ahead. He was sitting on a sack of apples and was proceeding in a very moderate gait, when the spirit of mischief inspired me to command him to halt.

The command seemed to galvanize him with a new and strange vitality, for he appeared to rise on springs to the height of a foot from the horse, and the quickness with which he jerked himself around to catch sight of the new danger threatened to dislocate his neck. What he saw did not satisfy him at all; for he evidently took me to be a rebel belonging to the vanguard of Forest's army. Up went his right hand, with a convulsive movement, to his hat, grasping it and dragging it rudely from its mooring; and while I repeated the summons to halt, and fired several harmless shots to enforce my authority, he whipped up his horse with the old beaver in his hand and dug his long heels into the animal's flanks; every instant looking back with an expression of fright which cannot be described. The more I called on him to stop, the faster he went, both ends of the sack bobbing up and down at a furious rate. I was well mounted, and could easily have overtaken him, but this was not my purpose. On he went, over four miles of road, reaching at last a block-house where some companies of colored troops were stationed. Here he paused just long enough to report that Forest and the devil were in full chase after him, and not a mile away; and then plying his hat and his heels with renewed vigor he shot out of sight in the dusty road beyond. A few minutes later I came up and discovered the ebony soldiers drawn up in line of battle at the block-house. The report they received from the messenger whom I had frightened out of his wits startled them all, and made them prepare for instant action. Some of the soldiers knew me; and when the story I had to relate was told, the guffaws that followed might have been heard a mile. Some hours later I reported at Pulaski that Forest had taken the trestle-works, designing to move at once on our headquarters. Acting on this information, Pulaski was placed in condition to stand a siege; and when Forest came, as he promptly did, the blow he meditated was not struck, and he moved off toward Columbia.

Meantime General Rosseau, with quite an army, was pursuing Forest through the country bordering on the Tennessee River. One day while at Pulaski Isaac Towny, one of our scouts, called on me, and said:

"Bill, five or six scouts whom I have sent with dispatches to General Morgan, who is about fifty miles from here, all have failed to get through. Now, I want you to try it, and if you consent I think my brother, John, will go with you."

I agreed to go and at the commencement of a very dark night John Towny, Britton and myself threw ourselves into the saddle and started with a dispatch for General Morgan's command. On our route south we came, about midnight, to the suburbs of Rogersville, where, as I was riding a little in advance, I heard sounds which indicated the presence of many horses in the village. I found out subsequently that two companies of rebel cavalry were there that night. I reined up my horse and turned to my companions, saying:

"There are rebs here, as sure as you live, and if we get through the town at all we must first drive them out."

Having concerted our plans we broke out all at once into a series of horrible yells, mingled with the repeated volleys from our pistols. At the same time we spurred our horses, being careful, however, not to proceed so fast as to endanger our little strategy by revealing the smallness of our force. The *ruse* was crowned with success, for, coming as it did, in the darkness, at midnight, and totally unexpected, the rebels were frightened into a panic, and left the town in a hurry.

When the coast was clear we passed through the town and continued our way up the Tennessee River. When near the place of our destination a Union officer and four soldiers were seen approaching us. It was now some hours after daylight. At first we did not know the character of the party about to meet us, and fearing they were foes we prepared for a conflict, resolving not to surrender ourselves nor our dispatch. Happily there was no need of fear; and in a little time we presented the message we had brought to General Morgan. After refreshing ourselves and horses we were directed by the general to take a dispatch across the country seven miles to General Rosseau, whose army was then marching along the military road. The dispatch was taken to Rosseau, who, in turn, gave me one to take to Pulaski. Before starting I received a recruit to go with us, in the person of a gallant young man named Bishop, whose mother, a widow lady, lived at Pulaski. Lagging in the rear of Rosseau's army, with a lame horse, was a soldier whose company we also obtained on this return trip.

It was some hours before night when everything was in readiness for the final start. There were five of us now in the party, all armed in good style. The country through which we had to pass was full of guerrillas and danger lurked all along the way. Bishop and myself took the lead, and we held our pistols cocked, ready for any emergency. My desire for the approach of night, so that we could travel with a greater feeling of security, amounted to a prayer. At length the darkness came, through which we moved in silence, till near the noon of night, when, in the gloom to the left, we observed a house on a hill, with a field and a high fence on the right.

Bishop and I were passing beyond the house when the three in the rear halted before it, and Towny called out:

"We are going to stop here for grub and, Bill, you and Bishop had better do so, too."

"No," I replied, "I must go on, now, whether you stop or not."

Leaving the three on their horses in front of the dwelling, we, who were in the lead, pursued our way. Some little distance ahead the road turned square to the right, around an angle of the fence, along which we were riding. Suddenly, and without any premonition, as we turned the angle, we found ourselves almost in the midst of a party of rebel horsemen, who had halted in ambush, having evidently heard our approach. It was a crisis in which the utmost quickness of thought and action was required. In an earnest whisper to Bishop, I said:

"Get back! get back!"

Supposing my friend would do as bidden, I wheeled my horse and fled with all speed on the back trail. I heard no commotion behind me among the rebels and never knew, until I was nearly back to the house, that Bishop was not close at my heels. The three boys were still on their horses, as I had left them, for the period of my absence must have been very brief.

"What's up, Bill?" demanded Towny as I dashed into his presence.

"Why, Bishop is taken," I replied; "and we must get back for our own lives."

All thought of grub was now forgotten; and our party now sadly reduced by the loss of Bishop dashed away like a torrent, while the signs of pursuit were beginning to be too manifest to be mistaken. At length we came to a path running into the road, along which we dashed regardless of all obstructions. What I saw and heard at the fence, although the darkness was quite deep, convinced me that the force of the enemy who had captured Bishop was greatly superior to our own; and it behooved us to get away without an engagement. I still retained the lead; and in the course of a mile or two, as we proceeded up the narrow defile, we came to a place which was bounded on one side by a high and precipitous hill, and on the other by a dense woods, filled with brush, and entangling grape vines. Here we tried to scale the hill, but finding it, as we believed, inaccessible, the effort was abandoned. We determined then to retrace our steps on the path, and form a junction again with the highway we had left. We continued some distance on this retrograde movement, when we were startled by the tramp of horses' feet on the very path we were treading, and right between us and the main road.

Manifestly, we were in a trap, like that of the Hebrews at the Red Sea, when Pharaoh was in hot pursuit. Back we went again on our tracks just made, until we arrived at the point where we had attempted to climb the hill. Here we dismounted; and being nerved by the gravity of the situation we clambered up the steep acclivity with infinite difficulty, leading and helping our jaded steeds as we climbed or crawled. We were not a moment too soon in reaching the summit, for our pursuers were closely after us; but the ascent we had made baffled them, and they turned to seek us by some better but more circuitous route. Off we went over the upland till at a convenient place in the forest we halted and remained on guard for the rest of the night. When the sun was up we renewed our toilsome journey; and after traveling two miles we struck the same road on which, though quite a distance away, the capture of Bishop occurred. Here we counted the fresh tracks of twelve horses, which were made, as we rightly inferred, by the party whom we had confronted.

Without further trouble we rode on to Pulaski where, after reporting to the general officer, I visited Bishop's mother and broke to her the sad tidings as gently as possible. Her grief was painful to witness. The hope of seeing her son again was her only consolation; but this hope was never realized. From the night on which he was taken by the enemy, until now, his fate has been involved in mystery. Not a word concerning him has ever reached his friends.

# CHAPTER IX.

### FOUR INCIDENTS.

James Holly—Rebels at Jumpertown—Pierce and his Company—Rebels in Line—The Signal Gun—The Traitor—Our Retreat—Scene at the Bridge—Capture of Pierce and his Men—Flag of Truce—The Guerrilla Chief—All Night with him—Lieutenant Gardiner—Parole of Pierce—Swim the River—The Man with the Portmanteau—Ten Thousand Dollars—Murphy—The Refugee—We Go to his Home—His Union Overcoat—Assault on his House by Guerrillas—Shot-gun and Revolver—The Fight from Door and Window—Defeat of Foes—Killed and Wounded—Expected Return of Guerrillas—Murphy's Sad Farewell and our Return to Corinth—An Old Rebel—Mischief against Him—Visit the Calvins—My Threat—Arrested as a Guerrilla—My Acquittal.

In the early part of my scouting experience I met James Holly, who was acting the spy for the sharp-shooters stationed near Corinth. He told me that rebels were encamped in force about Jumpertown, and suggested that a company should be sent to chastise them, or at least ascertain their numbers and position. It is well to explain here that Holly was playing a double part, being in fact a rebel, though in the service of our sharp-shooters.

It was arranged that a company of eighteen men, under command of an officer named Pierce, should be sent on this expedition. Holly and I were to precede this force, keeping about a quarter of a mile in advance, so that we might signal the soldiers when danger was imminent. The bridge on our most direct route had been destroyed by rebels, making it necessary for us to go by way of Jacinto. A long corduroy bridge extended to the suburbs of Rienzi; and we—that is, the two scouts ahead—were nearing the end of this structure when, casting my eyes forward through the foggy atmosphere I perceived a formidable force of Confederates drawn up in line and waiting to receive us. The whole thing had been well planned by Holly to betray us; and it succeeded only too well, as we shall see.

The space between me and the rebels, when I caught sight of them in the fog, was but a few rods. I fired into them; and having thus given the signal agreed on in case of danger I turned and fled, with Holly close behind. We were both mounted on racers; and had little difficulty in distancing pursuit. As I sped back to our soldiers I was surprised beyond measure to find Pierce off his horse, trying, with the help of others, to drag some of the ponderous logs away from the bridge, intending in this way to form a breastwork, or leave a chasm in the road over which the rebels could not pass. Exhorting him to desist from this absurd labor I kept on my course and escaped. Twelve men of the command, including Pierce, were made prisoners.

Next day, Frank Harrison and myself were dispatched south, under a flag of truce, to negotiate an exchange of prisoners, so as to secure the release of Pierce. Not far from Rienzi we saw before us five men, all of whom were rebels, or rather guerrillas, from their general appearance. Their leader, who was no other than the notorious desperado Thunderburg, wheeled his horse across the road, assuming an offensive attitude. We displayed our flag of truce, and it was respected. Thunderburg engaged in conversation with us, during which he inquired if we had seen a squad of Yankees cross Tuscumbia Creek that day. We answered in the negative; after which we told him our business and invited his assistance. He instructed us, in the most gracious manner, to proceed south, and in the course of an hour, as he had other matters just then to attend to, he would overtake us and give us all the help in his power.

True to his word, he rejoined us at the given time, and we rode on till dusk, when, at the forks of the road the four subordinates were dismissed, and we who remained wended our way to the residence of a citizen, well-known to our guide. Here the guerrilla chief and ourselves supped at the same table. So kind was he that he proposed to bring an officer that night with whom the exchange could be effected. He slept in the same room with us, and before day he was on his horse, seeking to carry out the purpose of our visit. After breakfast he returned with Lieutenant Gardiner, who informed us that our wishes in regard to Captain Pierce were forestalled, for he was already paroled and at liberty. We were told, too, that the captors of Pierce were bound to take his watch and other valuables, but they were restrained from doing so by Gardiner. Before we left a large number of rebels came to the house to see the two Yankees who were there. Our presence excited much attention and remark. At length, after thanking our host, the guerrilla chief, and the lieutenant for their kindness and courtesy, we took a respectful leave. Holly never received his deserts. He was partly punished, however, by a term at Alton, in the penitentiary. \* \* \* \*

On another occasion, I left Corinth and crossed the Tennessee River in a skiff, swimming my horse after me.

On the other side I scouted a day or two with some success in quest of Roddy's command. Returning I re-crossed the river and was within seven miles of Corinth, when I met a large and portly gentleman, who was toiling along the way, under the weight of a well-filled pair of saddle-bags, or portmanteau. He was walking and was evidently weary. I was wearing at the time a long jeans coat and a white wool hat, being habited in the main like an average Southron. In fact, no stranger would have suspected me, from my appearance, to be related at all to the Yankee race. I halted and accosted the stranger. A conversation ensued between us, during which he wished to know the name of the Southern general I was serving.

"I belong to Roddy's command," said I promptly. "I am just from there and am one of his scouts. By the way, sir, have you seen any Yanks to-day?"

"Yes," he replied, "I saw plenty of them at Corinth as I passed through the town this morning. I have no trouble in traveling among them, for I have a pass. I am going now to see Roddy. I was over there two months ago, swimming my horse as you did."

"I recollect you now," said I, with a start of sudden but assumed recognition. "I thought I had seen you somewhere; and now I know it was when you paid that visit to Roddy. I am very glad to meet you again, although you probably do not remember me, even if you saw me on that occasion. Perhaps you will not consider me impertinent if I inquire what you have in those saddle-bags?"

Before this unexpected question was addressed to him I had, in the most easy and natural manner possible, dismounted. I was standing near him, noting carelessly the effect of my words. He started visibly and turned pale, but made out to answer:

"That's a singular question to ask a gentleman, and a stranger, isn't it?"

"Perhaps it is," I responded, somewhat sternly, "but I believe you are a Yank in disguise, and may be a spy. I repeat it, sir, what have you in those bags?"

"Well, sir," he answered, with evident discomposure, "there are provisions and clothes in them; some shirts, I believe. I hope that is satisfactory."

"No: it is not," I enjoined. "It is my duty to inspect the contents of these bags, and I warn you not to make any resistance, for you will find it useless."

As I spoke my right hand was placed firmly on the bags, and the stranger made a vigorous but unsuccessful attempt to wrest them from my grasp. In a moment, however, he thought better of the matter, and yielded as gracefully as he could to the demands of the situation. He blustered a little, asserting that he was as good a Confederate as Jeff. Davis, and claiming, truthfully, no doubt, that one of his sons was paymaster in the rebel army, and another was captain of a rebel gun-boat. It never occurred to him to suspect that I was on the Yankee side of the great national question.

I took the bags and examined their contents in detail. A belt was in them which had been worn around the body, but which had been taken off for some temporary purpose and stowed away here. To my great surprise it contained ten thousand dollars, in one thousand dollar packages, all on Southern State banks. At the time of which I write the value of these notes in the South was not greatly depreciated. Besides these bills I found in a pocket-book, on the person of my captive, greenbacks amounting to twenty-five dollars. Altogether I had drawn a rich prize; but what was I to do with it? I could keep it all and release my prisoner, on his promise to preserve inviolate secrecy; but what was such a promise worth? After all, the best course was the honest one, and I took it. I then told the stranger, whose name was Lee, and who was a cross between a rebel spy and speculator, who I was and what I was. Hardly waiting to note his surprise and mortification, I placed the bags on my horse, remounted, and directing the captive to go in advance, we went on to Corinth, where he was lodged in jail. Some time afterward some Jews claimed the money and it was given up to them. Proofs being wanting against him the prisoner was at length set at liberty.

\* \* \* \* \* \*

A brave and good man, named Murphy, was driven by rebel persecution from his home in Alabama. He came north to Corinth and found the protection he sought under the stars and stripes. There I formed his acquaintance. After some weeks of sojourn with us he became anxious to see his family, from whom he had heard nothing since his hurried and melancholy departure. He invited me to go with him, both as company and protection, and I consented. We had about forty miles to travel, and the entire route was beset with bands of disloyal ruffians, with whom robbery and murder were common recreations.

We had accomplished without trouble the greater part of the distance, when nearly night we crossed Yellow Creek and ascended a long and gentle slope on the other side. A dense forest was on the other hand, and just as we reached the summit we caught sight of four mounted men, who were coming toward us on the road. We had good horses and might have made a safe retreat, but being well armed we determined to stand our ground and fight it out, if that was the dread alternative. My friend wore a long Union overcoat, at sight of which the advancing horsemen turned and fled at their utmost speed, leaving us victors of the bloodless field.

Laughing at the discomfiture of these cowards we continued our way a few hundred yards, when Murphy, who knew the country well, turned into a path, along which we rode through the twilight and gathering darkness, until we arrived at our destination. I shall not pause here to describe the joy of the meeting, of which I was a tearful witness. There are scenes on the earth which are too sacred to be profaned by the pen of the historian. Next morning after breakfast, at a moment when happiness was expressed by every countenance, and all of us were unapprehensive of danger, a sudden noise outside disturbed us, and drew our quick glances in the direction in which it came. A dozen guerrillas, all on horseback, and armed like so many pirates, were seen moving toward the house with the evident intention of carrying our home-fortress by storm. They were terribly in earnest, for they commenced firing before they reached the house, mingling their shots with a fierce demand on us to surrender.

What was to be done in this fearful crisis? As yet no one of us was injured; but how long this state of things would continue no one could tell. There were but two of us who could be depended upon in the conflict just commencing, and what could we hope to effect in an encounter so unequal? We resolved, however, to die in our tracks rather than to surrender; for death and capture meant the same thing, with these merciless scoundrels. Our weapons consisted of a shot-gun and two revolvers, all loaded and in good order. Murphy stationed himself at the door, which he held slightly ajar when he fired. I stepped to a window, which gave me a favorable outlook on the charging enemy; and puncturing a port-hole in a pane of glass, I took steady aim, and fired in unison with my friend at the door. Our shots were repeated so many times, and with such deadly effect that the guerrillas, who expected an easy victory, imagined the house to be filled with armed defenders. After pouring on us several broadsides, which took effect on the external walls, and on the outside of the door, they fell into a panic and scampered away, leaving two of their comrades dead on the ground. A third one was wounded, but he managed to get away.

It was our belief that the rebels whom we met the previous evening knew Murphy; and being aware that he was returning home, they went off and reported their information, thereby obtaining reinforcements with which to make the dastardly assault just described. Be this as it may, it was certain that Murphy could not remain in safety another hour on the premises. The wolves, though frightened off for a time, would surely come back with greater numbers, and glut their baffled vengeance. They might burn the house, but they would hardly murder the wife and children. The husband, if found, would surely perish. The entreaties of his family prevailed on Murphy at last to return with me to Corinth. Quick preparations were made, and the saddest of all farewells was taken. Whether a reunion between the separated ones ever occurred afterward I cannot say; but the husband returned, with a heavy heart, to Corinth, where he was again protected by the old flag.

\* \* \* \* \* \* \* \*

A prominent slaveholder, by the name of McKissock, living five miles northeast of Pulaski, was compelled, much against his will, to take the oath of allegiance to the Federal government. Knowing that the oath was very little respected by him, and wishing to test the extent of his nominal adhesion to it, I went one afternoon to his plantation. Not far from the house, and near a border of forest land, I saw a colored man busily engaged in throwing corn into a pen of hogs. Approaching him, in a weary and halting manner, assumed for the occasion, I accosted him thus—

"Well, uncle, I'm a badly broken down Southern soldier, as you see, out of pocket, and out of grub; and I want you to go to your master and tell him what I've told you. Ask him to send to me, if he pleases, something to eat, as I'm dying for the need of it. Be quick, uncle, and I'll stay here till you come back."

"I'll do it, massa," said the man, in a reluctant and hesitating tone; "but dis chile dunno about it. Massa's bery tickler dese times, he am, sho as you lib; 'sides dis, he am orful cross' bout strangers dat axes him for sumpin to eat."

It was evident that, like all the rest of his race, he had no love for Southern soldiers, or their cause; but, perhaps, he was as anxious as myself to embroil a master he did not love in difficulty with the true government, and possibly with this view of the case in his mind, he consented to do my bidding. After a little time he returned from the errand on which I had sent him. His face was pensive and downcast, and his voice was dolorous, as he said:

"I habn't fotched anything to eat, boss, dat am a fack. Ole massa jis cussed me for gwine to him at all. He wur orful mad, and dis chile was so skeered dat he got away quicker'n lightnen!"

I determined, in spite of this repulse, to go on still farther in the little campaign I had planned against the old planter, and so leaving the slave to his own reflections, I went over to the servants' quarters and held quite an interview with the inmates of two or three of the cabins. To all listeners I repeated the same story in reference to my condition, which had been rehearsed to the man at the pen, hoping by this method that one or more of the slaves would transmit the story, as it had been before, to their master. If any of them did this nothing came of it. They all asserted "dat de ole massa had tuk de oaf and was afeard to feed enny of de rebels."

I had been for some time in one of the cabins, when four colored men came in, to gratify their curiosity by a sight of the stranger, whose visit to them was now known to all. Full of mischief and reckless of consequences I regarded them sternly and said in a tone of command:

"Get your traps ready, my fine fellows, and be quick about it, for I am going to run you off south before the infernal Yankees have time to set you free."

The four slaves said never a word when this awful threat was pronounced, but in meek silence turned on their heels and walked gravely away. I observed, however, as they receded from the cabin to a point at which they supposed themselves to be unseen by the rebel stranger, they changed their walk to a rapid run, and were soon lost to sight in the surrounding forest. There was something suspicious in their movements, but I was not able at the time to penetrate their motives. My thought was that simply fear was at the bottom, and they were running to escape the doom that was impending over their heads. They knew what they were about, as the sequel will reveal. It appears that about a mile from McKissock's plantation there was an old mill, disused as such then, and occupied by a small detachment of Union troops. No sooner, therefore, had the four slaves, who heard my ferocious threat, withdrawn a little distance from the cabin, than they hastened with all speed to the mill and reported, with every grimace that fear could produce, the cause and nature of their excitement. The officer in command grew irate at once and dispatched a squad of soldiers to the servants' quarters with imperious instructions to take, dead, or alive, the insolent rebel who had created all this disturbance. The colored men went back with the squad, chuckling in their sleeves over the counter movement against me which they had so cunningly contrived.

Wholly oblivious of what was going on outside, I was sitting, in a careless attitude, near the fire, and employing the time in talking with the servants who were present in the room. All of a sudden a kind of scraping noise near by aroused my attention, and an instant after I saw, to my surprise, the points of a number of bristling bayonets protruding in through the crevices on each side of the chimney, which was an old-fashioned structure, peculiar to primitive log cabins. The weapons were so dangerously nigh my head and heart I recoiled instinctively, hardly knowing what to do in such an unexpected crisis. The presence of the bayonets was enforced by a loud demand for me to surrender, and then the light in the door-way was darkened by two or three burly forms, pushing their way into my presence and cutting off from me all possible retreat. The leader of the party came forward, and placing his hand on my shoulder with no very gentle grip, informed me that I was his prisoner. I called for an explanation, but instead of getting it in any courteous style, I was denounced as a guerrilla and as an enemy of all decent people. I was called a robber and a murderer, worthy only of chains, torture and death. During this tirade of abuse from Union soldiers I tried frequently to justify my conduct by revealing my true relation to our government, but every sentence I commenced was choked off by a slight thrust of bayonets, which punctured the skin in several places and made me feel that I had placed myself in a very unfortunate dilemma. In fact, my very life was menaced by our own men, who were resolved from the first to view me as a guerrilla of the worst character, and nothing on earth seemed to be able to shake their mistaken belief.

I was forcibly dragged from the cabin; and then being placed in front of my captors, they hurried me forward, every now and then hurling at me some abusive epithet, or touching me up to a brisker walk by the points of their sharp weapons. To add to my humiliation the colored men who had brought the assaulting party against me, went along, delighted to ecstasy at the success of their scheme to outwit the bold rebel. In a short time we came to the mill, where I was handed over to the proper officer for examination and punishment. The feeling against me was so strong and so unreasoning it was hard even to get a decent hearing; and when this was obtained it was harder still, if that were possible, to prove myself sound in my Union record. No one present knew me personally, and no one, therefore, was able to testify of his own knowledge to my real character. At last, it occurred to me, to ask the commandant if he was acquainted with a Union scout named Coslow? He answered he was; on which I asserted that I was a scout under Dodge with him. I also related circumstances which fortified this statement. The officer was at length satisfied, and dismissed me, saying as he did so, it was no wonder his men were deceived, for my appearance and general manner were more like those of a Texan ranger than a Federal scout.

## CHAPTER X.

### CLOSING ADVENTURES.

Run Down by Rebels—Leap from Horse—Old Colored Woman—Her Kindness—Sleep in Cotton-gin—Find Skiff—Escape—The Log and Bushes—Roddy's Army—The Rattlesnake—My Disgust—The Old Planter—The Three Daughters—The Little Strategy—The Brothers—A Miscarried Letter.

AT another time I was returning to Pulaski from a trip across the Tennessee River when a number of mounted Confederates saw me and gave chase. It was but a few miles to the river, and I hoped to gain it and cross it before I was overtaken; but the horse I rode was weary with long travel, and was unable to respond to the emergency. Looking back I saw the utter hopelessness of an effort to escape in this way; and finding a favorable place for the purpose just formed, I sprang to the ground, as the pursuers were almost on me, and fled into the bushes. The hunters were soon baffled, and after speeding through the forest for a considerable time I halted to rest.

Again I resumed the toilsome march, and was within a mile or two of the river, when I chanced to meet an old colored woman. The race to which she belonged could always be depended on, and I had no hesitation in asking her for what assistance I needed. I wanted food and some safe retreat from my foes, till such time as I should find means to get away from that part of the country. The woman told me her home was not far off, and kindly proffered to help me to the extent of her ability. She conducted me to a cotton-gin out in a field, somewhat remote from any house; and as it was now night I crawled into a cavity in this curious piece of mechanism and took up lodgings there for a lengthy period.

Faithfully and well, for eight days and nights, this benevolent woman supplied my wants and kept me from starving. After night-fall, when the chances for my detection were few and small, it was my habit to issue forth from the gin and wander about in search of the means to cross the river. Alternately sleeping and watching, and noting the sluggish hours as they passed, the days were spent in a miserable monotony. It was my good fortune on the ninth day to discover an old skiff on the bank, and frail as it was, I launched it and committed myself to the uncertain chances of a voyage in it to the other side. I safely reached the promised haven, and then struck out, with buoyant heart and elastic step, for Pulaski, forty miles distant. Without farther trouble I arrived there, feeling profoundly grateful to the old bond-woman who so kindly cared for me in my tribulation.

\* \* \* \* \* \*

While under General Stockweather I went on foot from Savannah to Bear Creek, a distance of about eighty miles, to spy out rebel movements in that quarter. Finding the locality of which I was in search I established myself for some hours at a place in the forest overlooking the adjacent road. An old half-decayed log lay there. With a knife I cut a number of bushes and inserted them in the ground near the log, so as to form what seemed to be a natural copse or thicket. Into the shade of these bushes I cautiously crept and assumed a position which gave me a fine opportunity to oversee quite an extent of the highway in both directions. For some time I remained waiting and watching, and at last the tramp of an approaching multitude fell on my ear. Directly the vanguard of a rebel army appeared in sight, followed by a number of regiments, all flying the colors of the slave-driver, the stars and bars of the Confederate States. I counted fifteen hundred soldiers who passed in turn my point of observation.

While the column was marching by a rattling and rustling noise near me attracted sudden attention, and turning my head I saw, with a shudder, a huge rattlesnake crawling from the ground to the top of the log. With a sort of dumb fascination I watched him as he slowly came toward me, with a lack-lustrous eye and a bleared and sinister expression. The dog-days were on us and their influence on him was very perceptible. The motive of his visit to me could not be penetrated. Perhaps he came out to sun himself, or, possibly, he was there like myself, to witness the grand military pageant just passing. He was within seven feet of me when he paused and remained perfectly motionless. His head was a fine target for pistol practice, but a shot from me was extremely hazardous, for it would very probably have brought the whole rebel horde down on me with a vengeance. I waited till the rearguard of Roddy's army passed out of sight, and then emerging from the bushes, I went on my way, leaving the serpent to his sunlight and his repose. I have a natural antipathy to snakes, and I honestly confess that the hour I spent in company with that monster I was in greater terror than if I had been beset by armed rebels.

\* \* \* \* \* \* \*

On one occasion, while traveling alone, I stopped near dusk at the residence of an old planter, not far from Hamburg. Though a stranger, my appearance was so much in harmony with that of a Southern soldier, whose character I personated, I was cordially received by the family. My horse was stabled and fed, and my own wants were abundantly satisfied. The planter and his wife were hospitable and courteous; and their three daughters, who were in the bloom of young womanhood, were polite and agreeable, employing the time in conversing with me on such topics as were mutually interesting to them and myself. In the course of this animated interview one of the young ladies desired to know to what Southern regiment I belonged.

"I have the honor, miss," said I, with cool effrontery, "to belong to General Roddy's command."

"I am so glad to hear this," exclaimed my fair questioner; "for it happens that I have two brothers with General Roddy."

I then inquired the names of these brothers and the number of the regiment to which they were attached. My unsuspecting listener gave prompt answer to my questions; and as soon as she did so I seemed to be startled by a great surprise.

"Why, bless my soul!" said I; " I know your brothers very well. I have met them very often. I have bunked with them, and fought by their side; and indeed there are no other soldiers in Roddy's command whom I know better, or prize higher, than I do these gallant brothers of yours."

This was enough to ingratiate myself thoroughly in the good opinion of these ladies and their delighted parents. In the fulness of his confidence the old planter imparted to me many items of military intelligence, which were converted to good use, on my return to headquarters. The evening was spent in the most delightful manner, the young ladies competing with each other in doing honor to their Confederate guest, who loved so well their soldier brothers. Just before we separated for the night one of them asked me if I would be so good as to take, on my return to camp, a letter from her to her brothers.

"Nothing would give me more pleasure," said I, somewhat amused at my own audacity. "But as I am to start before day, so as to cross the river before the Yanks have a chance to take me, you will not have much time to write, unless you rob yourself of sleep."

"You may be sure, the letter will be ready," said she smilingly as she retired from my presence. Next morning before day, while I was at breakfast, which had been ordered for my special convenience, the girl who had promised to write, came to my side at the table and handed me a letter addressed to her brothers, expressing, as she did so, the hope that the missive and myself would get safely into camp without being intercepted by the horrible Yankees. I placed the letter in my pocket; and after thanking her for her kindness, and bidding her to convey to her parents, who had not yet risen, my acknowledgment of their hospitality to a Southern soldier, I finished the meal, and getting ready departed from the house. My horse, saddled and bridled, was standing near the entrance with a servant near by in attendance. To elude all suspicion I took a direction in leaving the house, which would lead any one who might be a witness to my movements to infer that I was going straight to Roddy's camp; but the instant the mansion was lost to sight, behind an intervening forest, I turned about and rapidly made my way to Corinth. Often since then I have felt a pang of regret for the impositions practiced on the old planter and his family, and especially for that part of the little drama which referred to the letter; but when I reflect on the intelligence in the interest of our cause which I obtained by a pretense of being what I was not, my conscience was subdued to its customary repose. One thing is certain, however, that letter never reached its destination, but was worn into illegible fragments in the pocket of a Union spy.

\* \* \* \* \* \* \* \* \*

One evening, just at dusk, Colonel Cornine made a descent upon the Confederate forces occupying Tuscumbia, and sent them flying before him. After taking possession of the town I was ordered to prepare for a trip to Corinth, sixty-five miles distant, with dispatches. I left our lines and started on my lonesome ride through the darkness. Next morning, just as the rays of the rising sun were gilding the eastern horizon, I suddenly came upon a squad of seven or eight mounted rebels. They were riding leisurely along a narrow way cut through a dense growth of timber. I was riding at a lope, dressed in butternut, as usual, and as soon as I perceived them I put spurs to my horse, nearing them at a run, meanwhile yelling, "Yanks! Yanks! Yanks!" at the top of my voice. The Johnnies turned and made away at full speed. I proceeded on my way arriving safe at my destination.

# CHAPTER XI.

### THE HORRORS OF WAR.

Hood's Raid—Condemned Stock—Colored Exodus—Lost Children—Pontoon Bridges—Drowning of a Child—Reach Nashville—Hundreds Perish—Patience of the Colored Race.

PERHAPS the greatest local excitement which occurred during the war was caused by the aggressive march of the rebel army under Hood, from Atlanta to Nashville. General Stanly, with an inferior force, retreated northward before the advancing enemy. At Pulaski the excitement seemed to culminate; for thousands of colored men, women, and children joined themselves here to the retreating Unionists, all trying to escape from the great raider, who was marching swiftly after them, and hastening their steps by a constant roar of fire-arms in the rear. There were several places at which large numbers of these people had been kept and fed by our government; and when the raid began, and universal alarm prevailed, the condemned horses and mules were turned over by General Stanly to aid them in their hurried exodus.

The sight that presented itself, when these ex-slaves caught up their little effects of whatever nature, and started out in mortal terror on this disjointed and chaotic retreat will never be described. As many as five or six of them, large and small, and of both sexes, would pile themselves incontinently on one poor, sorry beast; and then, not being satisfied with this original outfit, they would attempt to carry with them an assortment of household goods, such as pans, kettles, bed, and bedding. It was impossible, however, for these poor people to carry all their earthly effects with them, or even a part for any considerable distance; for when the firing behind them grew louder and more menacing, they dropped their chattels one after another until nothing was left to indicate that they ever possessed any property in the world, except the dilapidated clothing they wore. Often, too, the infants with them, and children also of a larger growth, who were borne along on this tidal wave of fear and flight, fell to the ground from the parental grasp, and were trampled to death under the hoofs of a thousand horses. In some cases the poor parents would, by permission of the soldiers, consign their little ones to the ambulances to be helped on in this way; the result of which was that, in these instances, which were numerous, the children were never heard of afterward. The general confusion and terror were renewed at Columbia, where multitudes of these dusky fugitives became frantic with fear and attempted, all of them at once, to force the passage of Duck River, on pontoon bridges. The space occupied was too limited to afford them an easy transit; and demoralized as they were by overmastering fright, they rushed against each other with such violence and momentum that scores of them were crowded over the sides into the river and consigned to a watery death. One poor woman who had the care of a child not her own was so demented by fright she hurled it headlong into the whelming wave, nor paused to note its impotent struggle for life as it raised its little hands toward heaven in agonized supplication for the help which would not come.

When they reached Nashville their condition was not made much better, despite the fact that Hood was now out of the way, for he was repulsed at Franklin and his army was beaten into fragments at the State capital. The sick among these fugitives were rejected by the crowded hospitals, while the others wandered about the principal streets, or the suburbs, in quest of food and places of rest. Many of them, doubtless, died of hunger and exposure, and many more would have perished in the same way if the strong arm of the government, combined with isolated cases of private charity, had not interposed to save them. Possibly the thought of their new franchise of freedom, which had taken them so recently from the house of bondage, gave thousands of them a courage and a power of endurance which they could not, or would not, have possessed as slaves. Enough, at least, has been said of them in connection with this exciting retreat, to show, that, in the darkest days of adversity, they displayed a patience and a profound philosophy in suffering never illustrated to the same extent, and under like circumstances, by any other race belonging to the earth.

# CHAPTER XII.

### TRUE FIDELITY.

Minerva Perkins—Out of Money—At Athens—Down with the Typhoid Fever—No White Unionists—Three Friends—My Faithful Nurse—Her Sacrifices and Devotion—Recovery—Colored Troops at Huntsville—Send for Minerva—Chicken Pies—Restaurant Business Failure—Prospecting for Lead—Back to Des Moines—Send for Minerva again—Our Marriage.

DRESSED in Confederate uniform I was one day riding through the streets of Pulaski a few hours in advance of General Dodge's army, when I was observed by a colored girl, named Minerva Perkins, who was destined, in the time to come, to serve my interests in a vital sense, to the extent even of saving my life. Subsequently I met her several times, the result of which was a strong mutual friendship. In May, 1865, just as the war was closing, I chanced to be at Athens, Alabama, where I had been engaged for a time in a business which promised well in the start, but which in the end proved to be an unprofitable venture. In fact, it left me penniless; and to add to my misfortunes I was prostrated by a violent and lingering attack of typhoid fever. I occupied a room in a house owned by a Mrs. Lyons. Meanwhile the colored girl of whom I have made mention had come over to Athens and was living in rented rooms in the same house in which I was lying sick. Being acquainted I sent for her, knowing her to be an excellent nurse in cases of sickness, especially in typhoid fever, in which she possessed much experience. She promptly came at my bidding, and from the moment she made her appearance until the disease was subdued, and I was out of danger, she was a faithful and devoted nurse, to whom I owe the preservation of my life.

This spell of sickness occurred while I was still living in a hostile country. So far as my knowledge extended, there was not a white Union family in the town. Two men, with rebel sympathies, Mr. Sargent and Dr. Malone, and a Jew, whose name I have forgotten, were the only white persons who commiserated my misfortunes, or attempted in any manner to relieve my wants. The white element was so strongly against me my death would have been regarded as a popular blessing. For two long months I was blistered and consumed by malignant fever and involved more than half the time in delirium, and during all this time my faithful nurse kept ward and watch, day and night, omitting nothing that promised help to me in this direful extremity. She gave up all else to bestow her entire time on me, and when three physicians gave me up to die, and when her colored friends advised her to abandon me to the fate which seemed inevitable, employed her own remedies and waited on her patient with such steadiness of purpose and determined resolution that death for once was baffled and driven from his expected prey. She would walk half a mile, over a rough and precipitous way, often in the night, to secure a supply of fresh spring-water, for the patient who was tormented with continuous thirst. Often, when clouds were passing over the sky and the darkness was intense, she was lighted on her course to the spring by successive flashes of lightning.

I had no money when first attacked, and it was not long before the little fund possessed by Minerva was exhausted. In this extremity so fatal to the poor when sick, she sold her own feather bed, and other articles of great value to herself, to secure the means by which I was kept out of the hospital, and by which, also, the supplies of food and medicine were purchased. In the course of two months, through her kind ministrations, my health was so far re-established that I began to consider the course that I should take, in reference to business.

I went over to Huntsville, Alabama, where there was quite a large force of colored troops. For several days I took my rations as I could get them, and lodged during the night in an untenanted house. Learning that chicken pies would find ready sale among the soldiers, I sent for Minerva to come over and engage in this business. She did so, and being an expert cook, her pies found ready market at fifty cents each. There were days in which she realized more than twenty dollars in this way.

Meantime the prospect for myself, in regard to business, was not brilliant. I established a restaurant, and hoped, with the help of my friend, to make it a success; but it terminated in a failure. The soldiers who purchased of us, did so, to a great extent, on trust, designing to make payment when the government settled with them. When they were paid off they were not in Huntsville, but in St. Louis, to which city they had been ordered for this purpose. In this way all was lost, or nearly so, that had been trusted out, and the investment was gone, leaving me bankrupt and despondent. I then made a contract to prospect for lead, in a country in which a fictitious excitement had been started on this subject. All my labor ended in smoke, and in the spring of 1867, after having made an arrangement to send for my devoted friend as soon as circumstances would permit, I came north to my home in Des Moines. In August, of the same year, she followed; and then, as honor, and principle, and gratitude, all concurred in the step, although odium and popular ridicule were incurred thereby, we were married, and to this day I am not conscious of having done wrong. Though the blood of the Anglo-Saxon does not flow in her veins, she has been, as a wife, as faithful and devoted as she was in her own native South, when, through her watchful kindness and care, she brought back the bloom of health to my fevered and emaciated cheek, and encouraged me to hope and live.

# CHAPTER XIII.

### REMARKS PERSONAL.

My Relation to the Army—Enlistment—Detailed as a Scout—Furloughed—Return to the Army—Offered a Lieutenancy—Statement of Captain Griffith.

BEFORE closing this volume I owe it to myself, as well as to my readers, whose esteem I desire to cultivate, to explain more fully than has yet been done, the position I occupied in relation to the volunteer army. It has already been stated that my enlistment was in the Second Iowa infantry, and to serve as a scout was detailed from company D of that regiment. I did not re-enlist as a veteran, but at the end of three years Adjutant Campbell wrote to Gen. Dodge a cordial indorsement of my conduct and services as a soldier and a scout, and asked for him to secure for me a separate furlough, as a testimonial which these services, in his opinion, demanded. On receipt of this request General Dodge wrote to General Sherman substantially as the adjutant had written, and very promptly a furlough for sixty days was duly forwarded. I loved military life so well that five days satisfied me, and then I returned to the army. I was offered a first-lieutenancy in the First Alabama cavalry but declined it, because I loved the adventurous life of a scout more than I did the honors of promotion in the ranks.

In this connection I also wish to publish the following statement concerning my father and brother, made by Captain H. H. Griffith, of the First Iowa battery, to which they belonged:

"Wm. H. Callender, about 50 years of age, enlisted in the First Iowa battery in December, 1863, or January, 1864, and was left at Chattanooga, Georgia, in charge of company property in May, 1864. While there he sickened and died. He was, when I knew him, a trustworthy and competent man for any sort of duty.

"John Callender, son of the above-named William, was shot at and near the rebel works at Atlanta, Georgia, about the 1st of September, 1864. He was a young boy, about 20 years of age, and was never under arrest or under punishment of any sort, and deserved the good will of all his comrades."

www.ingramcontent.com/pod-product-compliance
Lightning Source LLC
Chambersburg PA
CBHW020137170426
**43199CB00010B/777**